D0983674

HARDY CHRYSANTHEMUMS

HARDY CHRYSANTHEMUMS developed by Alex Cumming in his gardens at Bristol, Connecticut. *Color photograph by F. F. Rockwell.*

Hardy
Chrysanthemums

BY ALEX CUMMING

EDITED BY

F. F. ROCKWELL

Revised Edition

THE AMERICAN GARDEN GUILD, INC., AND

DOUBLEDAY, DORAN & CO., INC., GARDEN CITY, N. Y., 1945

ACKNOWLEDGMENTS

THE MODERN version of the hardy chrysanthemum has brought a new enthusiasm and a greater meaning to autumn gardening in a large part of America, and its zone is ever extending. This can be attributed largely to the improvements brought about in recent years, all of which is gratifying to the author, who—with other chrysanthemum breeders—has to some extent contributed toward its betterment.

That there is a very great future ahead for the chrysanthemum is evident. The gardening public, while not yet fully aware of the usefulness of hardy chrysanthemums, is rapidly becoming so, and as the tempo of improvement continues, as it will, better chrysanthemums and better ways in which to use them will materialize.

Plant breeding on a commercial scale is seldom the result of the efforts of an individual. Its continued success will reflect the smooth working of a

ACKNOWLEDGMENTS

competent and sympathetic organization. This by way of sincere and grateful acknowledgment to my associates and assistants here at Bristol, whose loyalty has made it possible to continue this work in spite of adverse world-wide conditions.

My thanks also to George L. Blake whose intimate experience, success, and enthusiasm for the culture of chrysanthemums under protection are so sensibly evident in his contribution to this book—"Shade-cloth Culture."

ALEX CUMMING

CONTENTS

ACKNOWLEDGMENTS 7

FOREWORD . . . . . *Richardson Wright* 15

EDITOR'S FOREWORD 17

I HARDY MUMS IN THE GARDEN 21
    What Is a Hardy Chrysanthemum?
    Two Leading Types
    What Is a Korean Hybrid?
    Hardy Mums in the Garden
    Mums as "Pinch Hitters"

II HISTORY OF THE GARDEN CHRYSANTHEMUM . 34
    The Chrysanthemum—Its Ancient History
    Garden Chrysanthemums—Their Development
    The Early-flowering Chrysanthemums—Their
        Origin
    Garden Chrysanthemums — Development in
        America

III SPECIES, TYPES, AND VARIETIES 46
    Chrysanthemum Species
    Selecting Varieties

CONTENTS

IV   CULTURE   63
     Gardening Intensively
     Condensed Rules of Culture
     Culture in Detail
     Summer Care
     Winter Protection
     Lifting Plants Over Winter
     Chrysanthemums as Cut Flowers
     Garden Chrysanthemums in the South and Southwest
     Exhibition Chrysanthemums in the Garden
     Exhibition Blooms in Pots
     Watering
     Overwintering Greenhouse and Not-too-Hardy Chrysanthemums
     Propagating Exhibition Chrysanthemums
     Shade-cloth (Black-cloth) Culture
     Garden Chrysanthemums under Greenhouse Culture
     Cold-frame Culture
     Garden Chrysanthemums in Pots

V   DISEASES AND INSECTS   113
     Diseases
     Insect Pests
     Nematodes
     Insecticides and Fungicides

VI   PROPAGATION   133
     Propagation by Means of Cuttings
     Growing Chrysanthemums from Seed

VII   CHRYSANTHEMUM BREEDING   138
     About Plant Breeding
     Breeding Chrysanthemums

CONTENTS

Chrysanthemum Hybridizing
Pollinated Plants and Seed—Aftercare
Breeding Hints in Brief
The Importance of Records
Mutations

VIII REMINISCING 166
Korean Hybrid Chrysanthemum Type
Introducing a New Chrysanthemum
Pedigree Chart of the Single Korean Hybrid
Chrysanthemums
Pedigree Chart of the Double Korean Hybrids
Looking Ahead

IX RECOMMENDED VARIETIES 190
Single-flowered
Duplex-flowered
Double-flowered
Pompons
Cushion Type
Exhibition or Greenhouse Type

MONTH-BY-MONTH FLOWERING 197

INDEX 199

ILLUSTRATIONS

*(All photographs by J. Horace McFarland Co. unless
otherwise credited)*

Garden of Hardy Mums at Bristol Nurseries   Frontispiece

Facing Page

Hardy mums in the mixed flower border 30

In placing varieties, keep height in mind 31

Types of Korean chrysanthemums 46

Azaleamums for the front of the border 47

Original species of chrysanthemums 50

Indian Summer, good for massing 51

Caliph, of oriental hue 58

Dividing an old plant 59

Pot plants set out in June 62

Same border in September 63

Section of mum border in August 78

The effect of overcrowding 79

Moving full-grown mums to the border 82

The same, three weeks later 83

Pink Spoon, desirable for cutting 90

Pale Moon, lovely in bouquets 91

Growing mums under shade cloth (*Photos by George L.
Blake*) 98

Structure for supporting shade cloth (*Photo by George L.
Blake*) 99

Rose Glow blooms in September 106

Lavender Lady has made a great hit 107

ILLUSTRATIONS

Facing Page

Nematode (eel-worm) infested plant 114
Louise Schling, good landscape variety 115
Silver Moon, a charming single 122
Autumn Lights, hardiest of the bronzes 123
Propagation by cuttings 130
Pot plant from a cutting 131
Mercury, the first Korean Hybrid 138
Symphony, an early Korean double 139
Mums in a flower arrangement 142
"One-flower" arrangement of mums 143
Eugene A. Wander, a favorite for cutting 158
Bronze Spoon, effective in arrangements 159
Dean Kay, an extra hardy "Cushion" 162
Marjorie Mills, for low borders 163
September Gold 170
September Cloud and September Bronze 171
Pygmy Gold, earliest pompon 174
Ruby Pompon, unusual in form 175
Goblin, a perky bronze 178
Judith Anderson, a favorite "button" 179
North Star, excellent for a low hedge 186
Mrs. Pierre S. duPont, exceptionally rich 187
Burma, a glistening bronze 190
Fred Rockwell, gleaming copper (*Grayrock photo*) . . 191

FOREWORD

IN THE OLD days the man who "crossed" flowers
was called a hybridizer. Now he carries a much
more important title. He is known as a geneticist.
He is steeped in the lore of parentage. He knows
what characteristics certain given flower parents
will impart to their offspring through succeeding
generations. In order to create new hybrids with
particular characteristics, he must use the parents
possessing these characteristics.

This may sound complicated, but it explains why
the work of a geneticist of the caliber of Alex Cumming is important to the gardening world and why
it is that he has been so successful in the contributions he has made to it. He has narrowed his field
of investigation and experiment to a few plant
families, of which the most fertile has been the
hardy chrysanthemum. Not only has he introduced
new colors and new forms into this family, but he
has strengthened their fiber and given them a frost-

proof hardiness. Thereby he has extended the season of their flowering so that our Northern gardens are rich in color through the autumn.

This would seem to be work enough for one man. Now he has written about it. Here is an entire book devoted to the hybridizing, raising, and care of hardy chrysanthemums. In the words of the scientific world, it is a monograph, the first monograph on this subject. Unlike the general run of scientific monographs, it is brilliantly written, packed full of easily digested gardening information, and is guaranteed to open new worlds of hardy chrysanthemum beauty to all who read it.

RICHARDSON WRIGHT.

EDITOR'S FOREWORD

Most chrysanthemum literature has had to do with the growing of this ancient flower under glass for cut blooms. Until a few years ago the hardy chrysanthemum—called "hardy" with a mental reservation—was just another perennial, prized chiefly for its sentimental connection with the famous hardy border attributed to Grandmother. (The good lady must have been mighty industrious!)

Fitting indeed it is that the man who, more than anyone else, changed all that, who rescued the hardy mum from its garden state of innocuous desuetude and made American homeowners chrysanthemum conscious, should give us the first book to deal with the culture of modern garden chrysanthemums.

As was to be expected, Alex Cumming has done this job in a masterly way. The same painstaking thoroughness that has gone into the creation of the new chrysanthemums, making Bristol Nurseries synonymous with this flower the world over, has gone into this book, which is as practical as it is interesting.

Since the first edition of *Hardy Chrysanthemums* much progress has been made both in the development of this fine flower and in its use as a leading plant for gardens large and small. This book of Alex Cumming's has contributed, no less than his work as a hybridizer, to the position now enjoyed by his favorite flower.

With the present volume in hand, the most inexperienced amateur should be able not only to attain full success in growing his hardy mums but to find many and varied uses for the different types. By following Mr. Cumming's suggestions, he can add greatly to the attractiveness of his garden, especially during that all-but-barren period following the first autumn frosts. For this book—as well as for the lovely and serviceable new flowers he has created—we feel that the gardeners of America owe Alex Cumming a vote of thanks.

F. F. ROCKWELL.

HARDY CHRYSANTHEMUMS

CHAPTER I

HARDY MUMS IN THE GARDEN

Hardy CHRYSANTHEMUMS today hold a dominant place in autumn gardens because they can be depended upon to produce masses of varied color over a period of six weeks to two months. From late August until hard, killing frosts they deck beds and borders in white, yellow, deep gold, bronze, pink, rose, lavender, crimson, maroon, and darkest red.

Then, too, the modern hardy mums in their wide variety of size and of form—as well as of color— are unsurpassed by any other flower, at any season, for use as cut blooms. They lend themselves to all types of decorations and arrangements, and have the unusual advantage of remaining, after being cut, in perfect condition for days, often for two weeks or more. These good qualities would place them near the top of the list as cut-flower material at any time of the year. Coming, as they do, when other flowers for cutting are at a low ebb, or lacking altogether, they are indeed indispensable to the lover of flowers who wants to enjoy their beauty indoors as well as out.

In addition to these good points, a further reason —if one is needed—for the extensive use of hardy chrysanthemums in the garden is the ease with which they can be grown and the certainty of success with them if a few basic requirements for their culture are provided. In this respect they are, it is safe to say, far more obliging than many other garden favorites—such as roses, delphiniums, or dahlias.

In fact, so simple are the essential cultural requirements of hardy chrysanthemums as a class that they can be pretty well covered in a handful of brief *do's* and *don't's*.

Don't crowd mums among annuals or other fast-growing plants; don't plant them in either shady or stuffy corners. Don't plant in heavy tree shade, for greedy tree roots will be contending with the mums for food and moisture. For the same reason, avoid planting close to privet or barberry hedges— a mistake frequently made.

Above all, *don't regard your hardy mums as permanent garden fixtures, requiring no aftercare.* Even the sturdiest of hardy perennials (with very few exceptions) resent such treatment.

The first "do" is to provide your hardy mums with abundant sunshine and plenty of room to grow and breathe. Divide strong-growing kinds *annually,* early in the spring; less vigorous kinds every second season. When replanting, give a change of soil if possible—any soil that will grow good vegetables or annuals will serve for chrysanthemums.

Finally, be on guard against any wet spots where rain or snow water gathers and remains for any length of time. *Good drainage is essential.*

WHAT IS A HARDY CHRYSANTHEMUM?

Many a novice with a newly acquired enthusiasm for chrysanthemums—along with other flowers—expects to produce in his own garden blooms that compare in size with those seen in florists' windows and at autumn flower shows.

A search through nursery catalogues fails to reveal any varieties similar to these prize beauties. The truth is that these chrysanthemums do not belong in the garden; they are pampered greenhouse products grown under glass all season by specialists who know their every whim. Each plant is allowed to produce only a few blossoms—sometimes only one. These identical varieties in many instances, if grown in the garden in the usual way, would produce flowers no larger than those of many of the hardy or garden varieties.

For the garden, get garden varieties. There are plenty of them. Let them flower freely—the more blooms the better. The effect will be natural and a thousand times more colorful than that of a few giant flowers. Of equal importance, the display will extend over a much longer period.

The term "hardy chrysanthemum"—or, as more commonly used, hardy mum, for short—is employed to designate a varied group of chrysanthemums that now include many hybrid types that have resulted from crossing species and older horticultural varieties. In general, it marks the distinction between the florist's or greenhouse sorts and those which are sufficiently hardy to be grown out of doors and which bloom early enough to mature their blooms before killing frosts cut down the plants.

The term "hardy," as employed in connection with the chrysanthemum, must, however, be taken with certain reservations. Many of the varieties offered in catalogues for garden use are not reliably winter-hardy in the more Northern states unless planted where they get excellent surface drainage and given protection with adequate winter mulching. Some of them, to be perfectly safe, require the protection of a cold frame—a cultural detail that, fortunately, presents little difficulty.

The different *types* of hardy mums resulting from recent work in breeding have become so numerous as to be somewhat confusing to the beginner. What with Azalea-chrysanthemums, Azaleamums, Cushion-mums, Summer-mums, Candytuft-mums, Korean Hybrids, Arctic Daisies, and so on, it is no wonder that he is at a loss.

It may simplify the matter considerably if we group all the low-growing, hyphenated varieties under the general head of "cushion" mums. These, with taller-growing Korean Hybrids, form the two leading groups.

TWO LEADING TYPES

As to these hyphenated mums, I would point out that the Azaleamum is not even remotely related in any way to the azalea; nor the Candytuft-mum to the familiar flower of that name. They are true chrysanthemums, and, like the Cushion-mums and the Summer-mums, they are low-growing, densely flowered plants, and usually bloom early—some of them as early as mid-August.

Dense and low-branching chrysanthemums of this type usually produce stolons ("suckers" from the base of the plant) freely, and hence are very resistant to winter injury—a characteristic of all the "cushion" sorts. Another good feature is that they require no pruning or pinching to keep them where they belong; they are naturally compact and low growing.

These hardy mums have their limitations, however. Being extremely branchy, they are not particularly valuable for cutting, although some of the more recent varieties give promise of improvement in this respect. Even the hardiest of mums cannot be counted upon to flourish undisturbed for several years, though an occasional plant in a favorable location may do so. What usually happens is that new plants make a good showing the first year but do not flower so early as the catalogue description indicated. The second season the plant will flower earlier and be better in every way. In the third year, look out for deterioration, or even the complete disappearance of the plant—due to exhaustion. The remedy? This unfortunate ending could have been prevented by dividing the plants after the second season of flowering, and placing them, if possible, in a new location in good soil. Early spring, of course, is the best time to do this.

WHAT IS A KOREAN HYBRID?

In most nursery catalogues the hardy chrysanthemum section is devoted largely to Korean Hybrids. It is in this group that the modern large-flowered varieties, with their marvelous range of colors and flower forms, are to be found.

But just what is a Korean Hybrid? A decade or more ago, for a short time after the introduction of the earlier varieties of this type, it was not difficult to classify them quite definitely. The first crosses of the older hardy mums with the then recently introduced Korean species (*C. coreanum*) gave us the original "Korean Hybrids." These had large single flowers; many of them—such as Mercury, Apollo, and Ceres—are still popular.

Further breeding brought double and semi-double flowered varieties. Still more recently the old-fashioned small-flowered Pompons have come under this Korean influence. The chances are that any present-day introductions of hardy mums have some of the blood of the wild *coreanum* in their veins. And now Arctic Hybrids (crosses of *C. articum* with horticultural varieties) are adding new qualities; and *C. nipponicum,* recently bred into other types, brings better foliage and new color tints.

This blend-within-blend hybridizing has made species identification almost impossible, and the term Korean Hybrid becomes less and less definite. The practical solution to the question "What is a Korean Hybrid?" is to let the botanist or the breeder—who are the persons chiefly concerned with scientifically accurate definitions—do the unscrambling; and to accept these later-day creations merely as better hardy mums. Suffice it to say that in comparison with the kinds grown twenty-five years ago, these new mums are hardier, far more brilliant and colorful, and better garden plants in every way. Their blooming season now starts in late summer and lasts after practically all other garden flowers have given up for the season.

HARDY MUMS IN THE GARDEN

A rather meteoric development this, when one realizes that it has all taken place within the present generation and that within this period the garden designer depended largely for fall color on the hardy aster group, not on the chrysanthemum! In fact, I doubt if any other garden flower, anywhere, in so brief a period, has shown such great improvement at the hands of the hybridizers.

The modern hardy mums have universal appeal for the gardener because of their peculiarly wide adaptability. Few flowers can be used to such good advantage in so many different ways.

A generation ago such hardy mums as we had were so late flowering that freezing weather often mowed them down during their first week of bloom; they were weedy in growth and of a more or less uniform height; and the colors were few and dull. Now, with bloom from early August to late November; with plants from a foot to 3 feet tall; with an almost unlimited range of colors and color combinations, and with flowers in size all the way from the tiny buttons and Pompons to singles, semi-doubles, and doubles that compare favorably with greenhouse-grown varieties—now, indeed, the gardener has at his disposal "a hardy mum for every purpose."

Mass Plantings

Masses of color, so readily obtainable in the spring with many of the early-blooming perennials and bulbs, have always been a problem for the late summer garden. The modern hardy mum fills this need to perfection—the Cushion types for August to mid-September, and almost any of the others for later, not omitting the extremely effective singles, such as North Star.

HARDY MUMS IN THE GARDEN

The autumnal colorings of many of the newer varieties, especially the bronzy and golden ones, make them particularly suited to mass planting, especially so for more or less formal effects. In stylized city gardens, where every inch of space must be utilized, they are equally good for formal or architectural mass plantings. The raised terraces at Radio City, for instance, are never more impressive than in the autumn when massed with low-growing hardy mums.

In Borders

In smaller gardens, where space for solid masses of color is not available, almost equally dramatic effects can be obtained with moderate-sized groups (three to five plants) at intervals in a long border. Here low-growing, medium, and tall varieties, flowering early and late, can all be used—care being exercised, of course, to fit them into their proper places in relation to other plants in the border. The tall-growing hardy asters make an excellent background for medium early varieties.

Against Shrubbery or Evergreens

Very charming landscape effects can be achieved by planting groups or "drifts" of hardy mums where existing shrubbery plantings or evergreens will make suitable backgrounds for them. For this purpose one would select the hardiest, most persistent varieties, such as Autumn Lights, Goblin, and North Star. And as these plantings are usually viewed from a considerable distance, the colors should be such as will show up in good contrast to the background. White or light varieties, for instance, stand out well against evergreens.

Along Walls

The tougher varieties of hardy mums are well adapted to planting in locations where many garden flowers would not do well, or could not conveniently be cared for. Along walls, or on not too steeply sloping banks, such varieties as Acacia or Autumn Lights, or any sort that is loose and graceful in habit, will serve excellently as material to make a glorious display of color for late summer or autumn. This is particularly true in instances where such a wall or bank is at some distance from the house or garden, for the plants require but a minimum of attention during spring and early summer, and the foliage makes an attractive ground cover until the plants come into bloom.

For Edging and Low Hedges

The Cushion-type mums and other dwarf sorts have distinct advantages for use as low edgings for taller-growing plants, or for a large mixed hardy border. For bordering a walk or drive (as, for instance, where spring-flowering bulbs have held sway) no other flower is more effective. The branchy, dense-growing varieties, such as King

HARDY CHRYSANTHEMUMS of various types can well be used as accent points in a mixed hardy flower border.

By COMBINING dwarf, medium-height, and tall varieties it is possible to get a

Cushion and Coral Sea, can be used as temporary hedges; in fact, the "hedge type" of hardy mum, with trim foliage almost as attractive as box or germander through the early summer, is already in the offing for introduction.

A practical application for the average home came to my attention recently. In this case Autumn Lights was used to form a line between the vegetable plot and the flower garden. Within sight of the street, it stopped many a passer-by.

In Pots and Window Boxes

In formal gardening it is often desirable to use flowering plants in large pots as points of accent, either in the garden design, at the intersection of paths, or on steps. For this purpose the dwarf, dense-growing sorts, because of their exceptionally long flowering season, are unexcelled. When to be so used, the plants can be grown in pots through spring and early summer; or they can be grown in the garden and shifted to the pots just before coming into bloom.

This type, too, makes most attractive material for window boxes, either in solid masses—after earlier blooming material—or used with other flowers.

MUMS AS "PINCH HITTERS"

I cannot close this chapter on hardy chrysanthemums in the garden without emphasizing a method of employing them which is overlooked by most gardeners. I refer to their use as "pinch-hitting" plants during late summer and autumn in *any part* of the garden or grounds where other flowers have failed to make good, or where earlier-blooming kinds have left undesirable gaps in the planting scheme.

It is no trick at all for even the inexpert gardener to transplant mums in full growth, or actually showing color. This is because of the dense fibrous root growth, which naturally makes an excellent ball, plus the woody top growth, which does not readily wilt, or, if it does, makes a quick recovery. (See page 64.)

I know of a number of municipal park departments which feature each autumn a hardy mum display from transplanted plants, as a follow-up for bedding plants that have passed their best or have been destroyed by frosts in early September. The city of New Haven was the first, to my knowledge, to make large-scale use of chrysanthemums in this way. Here magnificent mass groupings serve as a gorgeous background to the rose garden in East Rock Park after bulbs and annuals have had their day. Radio City also demonstrates the feasibility of this late-summer planting with the display which thrills thousands of color-hungry mortals every day in spite of occasional November frosts and freezes.

The University of Chicago, famous for the chrysanthemums of Dr. Kraus's origination, demonstrates a rather original and certainly effective pinch-hitting job in the use of hardy mums as a late-season fill-up for window and terrace boxes. Here the added shelter of the buildings must afford considerable protection and tend to prolong the display almost into winter. If our city dwellers—and suburban dwellers, too, for that matter—would just adopt this practice, there would be a delightful contrast to the rather letdown effect after that first frost destroys the summer plantings.

So why not grow extra plants in some out-of-the-way spot to fill in conspicuous gaps around the home? While the foundation planting in itself may not be the place to grow chrysanthemums as a permanent fixture, certainly a few plants tucked in at summer's end would add cheer to the autumn picture. What a difference it would make if the neighborhood generally adopted the practice, which is by no means too visionary—neighborhoods are responsive that way.

CHAPTER II

HISTORY OF THE GARDEN CHRYSANTHEMUM

THE CHRYSANTHEMUM—ITS ANCIENT HISTORY

THE CHRYSANTHEMUM is indeed a plant of ancient lineage, with an origin far in the distant past. Its authentic history, however, can be definitely traced back to the Confucian era. It is not generally known that Confucius, most famous of all Chinese philosophers and scholars, was first a horticulturist and doubtless one of considerable discernment. Born in the province now known as Shantung, in the year 550 B.C., Confucius was the official "keeper of the herds and lands" for the chief of the district in which he lived. He writes, "The Chrysanthemum has its yellow glory," in his book *Li-Ki* (Ninth Moon), which treats largely of ancient ceremonies and institutions.

Korea, associated with much of our fine garden material of today, looms large in the history of the garden chrysanthemum—both the very ancient and the very recent—as we follow its development. It is a matter of record that in A.D. 386 seed of the chrysanthemum was introduced to Japan from a foreign country. That foreign country, Taik-tse, is now one of the states of Korea.

From this date on Japan played an important part in the development of chrysanthemums. Reference at this early date is made to the colors blue, red, yellow, white, and violet. The reference to blue, however, is difficult to account for, there being no color now in the chrysanthemum family that could, by any stretch of the imagination, be called blue. Porcelains and tapestries of that era, however, show representations of unmistakably blue chrysanthemums.

The original *Chrysanthemum indicum,* doubtless the progenitor of all chrysanthemums, was yellow. The name "chrysanthemum," derived from the Greek *chrysos* (gold) and *anthos* (flower), given the plant by the immortal Linnaeus about 1753, indicates this. Linnaeus at that date described just two varieties: one single, the other with double flowers. Evidently all previous improvements were strictly confined to the Orient. It is recorded that between A.D. 365 and 427 a Chinese scholar and horticulturist developed the chrysanthemum to such an extent that his city was named Chu-hsein (Chrysanthemum City) by way of honoring his accomplishments. That the Japanese horticulturists contributed much to its early improvement is also apparent. In the year A.D. 910 Uda, Emperor of

Japan, instituted the Imperial Chrysanthemum Show in the imperial residence in Tokyo, and the chrysanthemum was adopted as Japan's national flower. It is interesting to note that at this time the double form of *Chrysanthemum morifolium* first appeared, because it is highly probable that most of our double garden chrysanthemums descended from this variety.

GARDEN CHRYSANTHEMUMS—THEIR DEVELOPMENT

No attempt will be made here to follow the development of the chrysanthemum in all its forms, because we are concerned chiefly with garden types. So, passing over some eight hundred and forty-four years, we come to the year 1754, when the chrysanthemum was first introduced from the Orient into England. Evidently it did not immediately create much interest, because the original plants were lost. In 1795 the chrysanthemum was again brought to England, but this time by way of France. By 1824 it had not only established itself as a florist's flower but its culture had spread to the windows of the humble cottages and perhaps to the most sheltered spots in the gardens.

Let us here consider for a moment the men who were then so intent upon developing the chrysanthemum as a garden plant. The contributions of these early breeders, now long forgotten, were brought about under the most difficult conditions. Those early enthusiasts, with little equipment with which to work and with material which required the shelter of a glass house or protected frame, reflect a picture of persistence and ingenuity. Imbued with the belief that the chrysanthemum could be weaned away from the sheltering influence of the glass house, with the vision of the true plantsman they saw its possibilities. The unfaltering faith with which they faced their problem is a fundamental need, which neither time nor science will ever change where plant breeding is concerned. The breeder of today, as of that time, must be firm in the belief that any objective reasonably conceived is attainable. We of today owe these early breeders an everlasting debt of gratitude. At that early stage their problems were immeasurably more difficult than are ours and their contributions of tremendous later importance; full credit is due them for their accomplishments. The difficulties in seeding chrysanthemums, experienced by the early plantsmen, are well illustrated in Payne's *History of the Chrysanthemum*. He relates that about 1836 "an amateur raiser was so extraordinarily fortunate in his cultural methods that he raised upward of five hundred seedlings." These were sold to a nurseryman, and a good number retained their popularity until the sixties. The "extraordinary fortune" can be attributed largely to the fact that the amateur in question was a baker and that "he had trained his plants to the wall behind his ovens"—where, of course, conditions would be favorable for the setting of seed.

New Types

The appearance of new types is also of interest. Payne again refers to a Mr. Parks, who in 1824 imported from China a quilled yellow variety which he named Warata'h. This variety is credited with being the precursor of the Anemone type. Among others of Mr. Parks's importations were two of note: one described as a double yellow ½ inch in diameter; the other a double white not more than 1 inch across. Both were considered double forms of *Chrysanthemum indicum*. It appears that these were of the Pompon type, although the small chrysanthemum had not as yet been specifically classed as a Pompon. The first classification of chrysanthemums is recorded by Payne as being made some few years later by a Mr. David Munro, who enumerated forty-nine varieties in the four following classes:

Class I. Large or show, requiring protection.

Class II. Large or show, quite hardy.

Class III. Large or show, but produced sparingly.

Class IV. Small or late, not worth cultivation.

If Class IV refers to what were later classed as Pompons, it would appear that this group got off to a considerable handicap. Incidentally, the good Mr. Munro's opinion in this particular is not unheard of today.

Quoting from Payne again, in connection with

the Pompon type: "Upon conclusion of the war in China in 1842, Hong Kong being retained by the British and other territories being open, the Horticultural Society of London sent Mr. Robert Fortune over to collect rare or unknown plants. Returning in 1846, he brought, with other choice material, two small-flowered varieties—one known as the Chusan Daisy, the other as Chinese Minimum. The latter produced but little seed; the former seeded freely the first year, and the seedlings from their compactness and resemblance to a rosette received the name of Pompon."

In spite of the confusion in small-flowered types appearing in various places about this period, there is every evidence that these two were the prototypes of all Pompon varieties.

Single Chrysanthemums were apparently ignored by those European breeders, for there is no reference to this lovely type, doubtless because the early development was away from the single, the aim being increased doubleness. The origin of the Anemone, Pompon, and Double types, however, is thus fairly well indicated.

THE EARLY-FLOWERING CHRYSANTHEMUMS— THEIR ORIGIN

The actual origin of the distinctly early-flowering type is of much interest. It is to France that we must turn for the record of its inception, so let us see just what progress the several French breeders were making up to the year 1850. There was indication then, as now, that earlier-flowering garden kinds were sorely needed. Payne dwells on the efforts of a M. Lebois who "had vainly sowed and sowed without obtaining anything to reward him that flowered before the fifteenth of October." He recounts further that "he exposed plants in the broad open sunshine, trained them to an espalier facing the south, cultivated them under glass, and even in a stove house, but still he could only bow to the invincible will of the plants which failed to flower early." It is not difficult to sense that M. Lebois about this time was a very discouraged individual!

Then, presto! Two seedlings were received from a compatriot, a M. P. Coindre, head gardener of the town of Avignon, France, "that were in full bloom as early as the month of August." From these plants two hundred seeds were secured. Sown in February, they flowered early that same autumn and "nine distinct double early sorts were selected." So enthusiastic was the worthy Lebois with his good fortune that his breeding efforts for several years after were confined to this group. Undoubtedly, then, the early-flowering type, for which we are all grateful, came into being at this period. Exactly how these two first seedlings were obtained by M. Coindre is not made evident. It is more than probable that an accident of nature brought about the very thing that M. Lebois could not accomplish in spite of his indefatigable efforts. Horticultural history tells of many of these sporadic mutations, occurring from time to time, without the assistance of man.

GARDEN CHRYSANTHEMUMS—DEVELOPMENT IN AMERICA

Brought first to America in 1847, it would appear that the chrysanthemum, while taken up enthusiastically as a greenhouse subject, had not made much progress gardenwise during the last century. The sturdy Pompon (more often called Artemisia in Grandmother's time) was, however, used in gardens to some extent. There is little doubt that Pompons reached our shores through the old mariners, many of whom were interested in plants. These varieties were hardy but lacking in bright colors. Being very late in flowering, they needed shelter or protection to shield the opening blossoms from the icy autumnal blasts usual in New England and other cold regions. Seemingly Grandmother's redflannel petticoat was often requisitioned to provide the needed covering. The red petticoat has so often been mentioned in this connection that one wonders if it had some special virtue or if it just happened to be one of the more abundant garments of that time. In any case it certainly would be unfortunate if our chrysanthemums today depended for protection upon that expedient—the habiliments of this generation would be of rather dubious value.

Development of the Pompon type forged ahead rapidly about twenty-five years ago, when it proved to be profitable as a greenhouse crop in the United States. The enormously large flowers of the exhibition type, having held sway for years, evidently had about reached their zenith in popularity. Public demand veered gradually to the smaller Pompon type, which was less expensive and much more practical as a cut flower. Breeders, quick to see the demand for better kinds, produced them rapidly; consequently, even new varieties were soon superseded. Many of them, however, escaped to the garden. It is unfortunate that names were lost in this hurried shuffle, because a number of these greenhouse discards had decided garden value in some sections of this broad land. As a consequence they have reappeared under various names; hence, the impossibility of accurate identification in many of these earlier sorts.

Early-flowering Double Chrysanthemums

The early-flowering Double type, always susceptible to the New England conditions, came into more general use about 1910. Nonin & Sons, the famous French exporting nursery, about 1900 began the introduction of an early-flowering and somewhat hardier set. Some thirty-two new kinds were catalogued, one of which was Perle Chatillonaise. In 1904 Normandie, Aquitaine, and Eden were offered with several others. The four mentioned varieties, still in circulation, are excellent where climatic conditions are not severe. It is from this group that a great many of our present garden varieties were developed. The development of new chrysanthemums, once under way, made rapid progress in America.

Some of Our Own Breeders

Prominent among breeders and distributors of garden chrysanthemums here are the names Dreer, Totty, Smith, and, more recently, the Bristol Nurseries, the latter particularly since their introduction of the Korean Hybrid type.

Charles Totty, Madison, New Jersey, long a pioneer in the dissemination of greenhouse varieties and an outstanding exhibitor, originated and distributed many fine garden kinds. The diversity of Mr. Totty's offerings will indicate the wide horticultural ability and knowledge for which he was noted. Fortunately, Miss Helen Totty of this firm is continuing in her dad's footsteps and doing a good job of it.

The firm of Dreer, Philadelphia, has taken a leading part in popularizing garden chrysanthemums. Eugene H. Michel, largely responsible for most of the Dreer varieties, is a firm believer in letting Nature follow her penchant for variation. Rather than resort to artificial pollinization and the multiplicity of detail which that method involves, he takes seed from selected parents, grows many thousands of seedlings, and then selects rigorously. His keen judgment is reflected in the early-flowering group of Korean Hybrids recently introduced, also many other meritorious varieties.

Among all American breeders, however, the late Mr. Elmer D. Smith, Adrian, Michigan, was unquestionably an outstanding figure. It is a fact that the majority of the large commercial greenhouse varieties leading the procession today are the product of his remarkable skill and insight.

Reference has been made here to the fact that in the ancient history of the chrysanthemum the city of Chu-hsien had been named to honor the greatest horticulturist of that day. It is fitting, then, that the city of Adrian, Michigan, as a tribute to Mr. Smith, adopted the chrysanthemum as its official flower. Adrian has long been recognized in horticultural circles as the cradle of fine chrysanthemums, and it can well take its place as the Chrysanthemum City of America.

Mr. Smith, whose first-named variety, Flora McDonald, was introduced in 1890, consistently kept accurate records of his crosses, which doubtless had much to do with his ability to turn out better chrysanthemums year after year.

Korea Again Contributes

Korea, mentioned previously for its prominence in connection with chrysanthemums in the remote past, again enters the picture at this late day. The

Korean Hybrid type, which the writer had the good fortune to originate, has contributed considerably to the present tremendous popularity of the garden chrysanthemum. The native Korean chrysanthemum (*Chrysanthemum coreanum*) is a remarkably hardy wild species, with white daisy-like flowers. For some unknown reason this species has only recently come to light. It is the dominant parent in the development of the more recent Korean Hybrid type, the introduction of which definitely associates Bristol, Connecticut, with the development of garden varieties.

With garden varieties only in mind, and merely as they concern the *American* garden, if the varieties and colors available twenty-five years ago are compared with the brilliant assortment developed since, then it can be said truly, I believe, that a greater advance has been made in this last quarter century than in any like period of a history that dates back to the days of Confucius.

Thus—perhaps rather sketchily—is the story of the development of the garden chrysanthemum brought down to date.

CHAPTER III

SPECIES, TYPES, AND VARIETIES

THE present classification of the chrysanthemum, particularly as it applies to the garden type, is insufficient. Through the intercrossing and blending of the various types, intermediate forms have appeared, such as Amelia (Pink Cushion or Azaleamum) ; and again varieties that are neither single nor double are so numerous that some revision seems needed. For garden purposes, however, if we eliminate the large Japanese and commercial greenhouse types, the following would hold garden dominance in about the order given.

Large Double Type

Full double flowers, 3 inches or more across, many of which are similar in form to the familiar double China aster. Still the most popular type. The recent introduction of the Korean strain to this group—as in Indian Summer, Romany, and The Moor—has brought new color tints and some added

TYPES OF **Korean** Hybrid chrysanthemums. The range in color is as great as that in size, form, and doubleness.

AZALEAMUMS—and other low-growing types now available in many colors— make excellent front-of-the-border material.

hardiness. Considerable further improvement is probable.

Single Type

One or more rows of petals, with a central disk or eye showing prominently. Recent additions, particularly in the Korean Hybrid group, including new color tints, delightful fragrance, better growing habit, and good keeping qualities when cut, have done much to increase the popularity of this group.

Duplex Type

Not included under existing classification, but could indicate a type in between the Single and Double types; i.e., informal flowers that have more than two rows of petals but still show a definite center.

Pompon Type

Small rounded blossoms, usually of perfect form, ranging from miniature button-like blossoms, as in Bright Eyes, to the large ball-like flowers best exemplified in Lillian Doty. The Chrysanthemum Society of America classifies this type in these groups:

Button, flowers not exceeding $1\frac{1}{2}$ inches in diameter

SINGLE

DUPLEX

FULL
DOUBLE
OR
DECORATIVE

TYPICAL
SINGLE
KOREAN
HYBRID

48

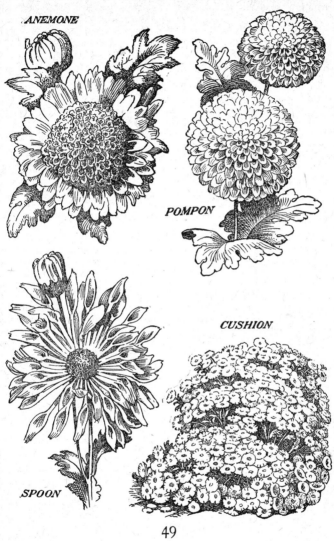

ANEMONE

POMPON

CUSHION

SPOON

Intermediate, flowers not less than 1½, nor exceeding 3, inches in diameter

Large, flowers not less than 3, nor exceeding 4½, inches in diameter. (This largest size applies to disbudded Pompons)

The Pompons are not so popular as the preceding types; nevertheless they should be included in every collection. They are more serviceable and have a greater ability to resist frost than the other types. To the New Englander particularly, where the Artemisia was a favorite in Grandmother's garden, this Pompon group will always carry a sentimental appeal.

Cushion Type

While there is no type so specified officially at present, there is little doubt that the increase in varieties of the Amelia habit of growth will warrant the adoption of a definite classification. They are distinctly cushion-like in their dwarf, dense, mound-shaped growth and fit into the garden where the taller kinds do not.

Anemone Type

One or more flat rays of perfect petals but with a pronounced cushion or disk in the center of the flower. So far this type, grown largely under glass, has been of little value to the garden, particularly in Northern areas, because the blossoms lack re-

ABOVE, original species, *Chrysanthemum indicum*. Below, the dainty, small-flowered species *C. morifolium*.

INDIAN SUMMER, in rich autumn tints, a fine variety for mass effects. Like Ember, it is exceptionally frost resistant.

sistance to inclement weather, and with few exceptions flower too late. However, a most interesting development has just recently come to light in the garden of Louis Reichert, Bellport, Long Island. Mr. Reichert's garden, within a few hundred feet of the Atlantic, appears to be particularly favored, for it simply teems with seedlings produced by Mother Nature alone. Never have I seen chrysanthemums grown under happier circumstances—healthy plants, flowers everywhere, color at its very best.

Mr. Reichert took up the hardy chrysanthemum as a hobby with the introduction of the first group of Korean Hybrids, which apparently seeded freely. Through careful selection of the seedlings he has developed some very interesting true Anemone-type varieties. The first of these to be introduced is named Korean Princess (Plant Patent No. 640). Coming from typically hardy parents rather than from greenhouse sorts, Korean Princess may prove the forerunner of a much-needed garden type. Mr. Reichert modestly ascribes this development to pollen-carrying insects, the ocean breezes, and generally favorable conditions, but there is ample evidence of intelligent guidance and good practice throughout his entire garden.

Cascade Type

A recently introduced group, usually with numerous small or medium-sized single blossoms.

The growth is more pliable than usual, and the plant may be trained to droop or hang down; hence the term cascade. Any chrysanthemum that will respond to this type of training may be included in the group. None cascade naturally. Desirable for pot culture, particularly as large specimens. Of possible garden value in Southern latitudes.

Spoon Type

Also a recent addition, characterized by long tubular petals, terminating in a flat, spoon-like tip.

CHRYSANTHEMUM SPECIES

The related species, of which there are many, are with few exceptions of little garden value. The majority are too weedy for the average well-kept garden and would doubtless be of interest only to the student of botany. A number would be at home only in the wild or semi-wild garden. It is not our intention here to go into detailed classification but rather to refer briefly to those which are of value from a garden standpoint or for breeding purposes.

Chrysanthemum hortorum

Not a species or type, but mentioned here to avoid possible confusion. The term refers to any cultivated chrysanthemum supposedly derived from interbreeding the species *indicum* and *mori-*

folium. In practical usage it includes any variety, other than the Korean Hybrids, that is useful for garden culture, regardless of type.

Chrysanthemum arcticum (Properly Chrysanthemum yezoense)

From Arctic Europe, Asia, and America. A species of low, mound-like growth, seldom exceeding 15 inches in height. It is remarkably hardy and somewhat deciduous in character. The wood of the previous season will often produce new bud growth, shrub-like, after surviving a winter temperature of 20 degrees below zero. Attractive single flowers, 1½ to 2 inches across; white, shading from light to deeper pink when mature. Good in the rock-garden background and in the hardy border; also desirable for bank planting.

Arcticum breeds less readily than *coreanum* but it is now being used to good purpose, particularly by Vincent DePetris, Detroit, Michigan, who recently introduced a group of well-chosen and well-named varieties, including Coral Sea, Arctic Queen and Dubonnet, all of which are rugged growing, hardier than average, and withal very lovely.

The fact that this skillful breeder, who already has many fine greenhouse varieties to his credit, now has the Hybrid-Arctic group under breeding control is a definite promise of more and better garden chrysanthemums to come.

The popular Northland Daisies developed from

Astrid—a natural garden hybrid from *arcticum*—by Mr. and Mrs. Franklin Styer, Concordsville, Pennsylvania, differ from the DePetris type somewhat, branching from the stem rather than the base, and being slightly taller and later in flowering. The Styer hybrids are all very hardy too. Several of the Bristol Nurseries' introductions (Autumn Lights in particular) have more or less of this *arcticum* parent to some extent in their make-up.

Chrysanthemum coreanum (Korean Daisy)

Native of Korea and north to Siberia. Similar in appearance to *arcticum* but taller, often attaining a height of 3 to 4 feet when mature. Single flowers 2 inches across; open pure white, changing to pink, with occasional carmine-pink tones when mature. Chaste and beautiful as a background plant and particularly effective against evergreens. Brought to America by E. H. Wilson and planted in the Arnold Arboretum. Here it attracted the attention of Harlan P. Kelsey, a true plantsman and great horticulturist, who introduced it in a commercial way. *Coreanum* is the dominant parent of the Korean Hybrid strain originated by the writer. Occasionally the question is asked, "Has not the garden chrysanthemum been developed to about its limit?" Right here I can say most emphatically, "No." This group, as an example, offers endless possibilities. The influence of this Korean Hybrid strain has already made its impression on the garden chrysanthemum although as yet the surface is no more than scratched.

Chrysanthemum coccineum (Colored Daisy), *Pyrethrum coccineum* or *roseum*

From Persia and Caucasia. This is the familiar *Pyrethrum hybridum* of commerce. Interbred with the garden chrysanthemum, it has proved of value as a pollen parent; although hybrids so far have been dominantly chrysanthemum. Some extremely desirable color shades have developed; also a greater depth of richness in the crimson shades has been achieved. *Coccineum* is not susceptible to the insects which malform and largely destroy most early hybrid chrysanthemums. If this resistance can be transferred in part, that alone will be most desirable. The Urchin, an odd but interesting and not unattractive hybrid introduced in 1937, is the first-known hybrid to be produced. A casual inspection of the foliage and peculiar stool formation of the crown readily verifies its parentage. Some very lovely hybrids, with large double flowers and delightful color blends, will soon be available. To the breeder this group offers promising possibilities.

Chrysanthemum maximum (Shasta Daisy)

There appears to be little affinity between this well-known group and the chrysanthemum. As a pollen parent it has been used to some purpose, but hybrids so far lack hardiness. Numerous variations developed, however, show interesting possibilities; particularly in the direction of a more compact and earlier-flowering type that may attain real garden value.

Chrysanthemum morifolium (Florists' Chrysanthemum)

From China and Japan. The original type carried small single flowers, varying from white to pink or lilac, with a prominent yellow disk. The form now generally offered is rosy lilac with lavender shadings. Attaining a height of 2 feet, with many slender lateral growths, it forms a graceful and most attractive plant, but unfortunately it is not sufficiently hardy for general outdoor culture. A double form appeared about A.D. 910 which doubtless was a progenitor of most of the present double sorts. *Morifolium,* however, has not, in the writer's experience, proved a desirable type for breeding purposes.

Chrysanthemum nipponicum (Nippon Oxeye Daisy)

From Japan. Distinct from all the other mentioned species in that it is shrub-like, with woody, deciduous stems, a large part of which will overwinter and produce new lateral wood in spring. The thick oblong leathery leaves have a texture that is unusual. Flowers are single, 3 inches or more across, and pure alabaster white when properly finished; greenish white under poor conditions. Far from pliable as a parent, it is finally proving valuable. Its heavy petal and leaf texture has been to some extent imparted to Milky Way and Burma as well as many other hybrids in the making. New tints of bronze and orange, more luminous, characterize many of the hybrids.

Chrysanthemum uliginosum (Giant Daisy) Pyrethrum uliginosum

From Hungary. An erect-growing type attaining a height of 6 feet in the rich, moist soil which it prefers. Flowers are single, 2½ to 3 inches across, pure white, occasionally tinted pink when mature. Flowering in late August and September, it is a valuable background subject for the hardy border or semi-wild garden. Efforts of the writer to cross this species with the garden chrysanthemum have been unsuccessful, which may indicate either an entire absence of affinity and that it is a true pyrethrum, or that just the right combination has not yet been used.

Chrysanthemum indicum

Native of Japan and China. Miniature pure yellow, single blossoms, seldom more than ½ inch across, are carried on dainty sprays in the utmost profusion. While not hardy enough for New England conditions, it flowers early—about late September—and could be carried over in a well-protected cold frame. Lovely enough to merit a trial in the wall or rock garden. Grown in pots, it responds readily to cascade treatment. It is difficult to believe that from this tiny little blossom the wide range of garden chrysanthemums and the enormous exhibition types of the florists were largely developed. Acacia, a hybrid of *indicum* and very similar to it is, peculiarly enough, hardier than the majority of garden mums.

SELECTING VARIETIES

In selecting varieties for the garden, one should be governed first by conditions in the immediate locality, particularly in Northern latitudes. Altitude also is an important consideration. Varieties that are good in the more temperate regions of the North Atlantic states, including New Jersey and Maryland and parts of New York and Pennsylvania, are not necessarily good in New England. Cold "pockets" prevail in many parts of New England and elsewhere, making it difficult to flower successfully sorts that may be seen flourishing even farther North. This also has a direct bearing on hardiness. In choosing from catalogue descriptions, do not overlook the fact that information pertaining to flowering dates and hardiness usually refers to the section from which the catalogue emanates.

CALIPH, one of a group of doubles in rich oriental shades, such as The Moor, a lively crimson, and Mandarin, glowing coral and copper.

APRIL DIVISION of an old plant: the four larger divisions, containing three shoots, will make oversized plants; the single-stem divisions are large enough to develop good flowering plants. The middle or "core," at the center, is worn out and should be discarded.

SPECIES AND VARIETIES

It is now possible to obtain varieties that will flower as early as July. The question arises, Do we want chrysanthemums at this period, when there is such a plentiful supply of more seasonable material? It should be kept in mind that there are many insects, such as cinch bugs, lace flies, grasshoppers, and others, that either eat or sting the tiny buds then in the process of development. Consequently, the earlier flowers are very apt to be malformed. Moreover, they are usually lacking in color.

The cool nights and brisk days of late autumn seem necessary for perfect development of the chrysanthemum. By this time the more troublesome insects have disappeared, and the color improves with the approach of frost. The logical time, then, for a fine display of bloom would seem to be just when the less-hardy annuals, such as heliotrope and zinnias, are likely to be destroyed by the first killing frost. This particular period varies greatly throughout New England. October 1 to 5 would be a reasonable average. It depends less on latitude than on altitude or on the proximity to the seashore or large bodies of water. The selection of varieties that are showing color well by this time assures a full chrysanthemum season.

In regions where the summer season is short and early frosts prevail, earliness in flower is of first importance. Varieties are indicated elsewhere that will be found desirable under these conditions.

Hardiness

Hardiness of the variety is of decided importance but is difficult to determine. Having in mind recent winters, during which many trees and shrubs were injured and even plantings of Bearded Iris were killed outright, it would be rash to state that any chrysanthemum variety is absolutely hardy.

As previously noted, local conditions seem to be the dominating factor. Seldom is extreme cold in itself responsible for winterkilling, which may be caused by a soil that is soggy or wet over a considerable interval. Shallow-rooted, half-starved plants are, of course, susceptible. The alternating freezing and thawing of mild winters exact the greater toll. Numerous tests conducted throughout the country indicate the perverseness of the chrysanthemum where hardiness is concerned. The species *arcticum,* as an example, overwinters perfectly in Connecticut even when the temperature has passed the 20-below-zero mark, killing shrubs and fruit trees. Again, it has overwintered in mild winters when thawing and heaving have injured not only perennials considered entirely hardy, but well-established shrubs and evergreens. In tests made at the Ohio Experiment Station during the winter of 1935–36, this sturdy *arcticum* species was all winter-killed; whereas varieties such as Normandie and October Girl, neither of which is more than half hardy in Connecticut, proved entirely hardy!

I would point out that breeders are constantly striving for that perfection in a variety which will combine all the good qualities—better color, improved form, earliness, and hardiness.

In the sense in which the term "hardy" applies to any herbaceous plant, it can be said that many of the newer kinds are hardy and also early flowering enough to assure a gorgeous display before killing frost. With reasonable protection and winter care they will survive average conditions.

Frost resistance in the open flower is another rather important factor. Certain varieties that are reasonably hardy otherwise will suffer injury when in full bloom if the thermometer nears the 32 point. A sharp frost at this time may temporarily spoil a perfect display until the partly opened buds bring color again. This is particularly true of the white and light-pink varieties. The bronze and deeper shades appear more frost resistant, as do also the double kinds in comparison with the semi-double and single types.

Gardening Kinship

The beginner would do well to consult with local nurserymen or specialists for definite information concerning varieties. Neighboring gardens also should be visited. In this connection, the writer, when noting a plant or variety of special interest in a strange garden, has never hesitated about approaching the owner or gardener as to its identity.

Never has there been any intimation that such a visit was considered an intrusion nor has there been a lack of welcome. The true garden enthusiast is quick to recognize a common interest. There exists a kinship among plant lovers that seems to be all-sufficient. In this way friendships are established and much worth-while information is secured.

"BIG PLANTS from little cuttings grow." Little tots, from 2½-inch pots, set out in early June. By looking carefully you can make out one of them just above the label stake! (*See illustration on following page.*)

AND HERE THEY ARE in mid-September! Pygmy Gold is the variety—a Pompon Korean Hybrid designed for summer bedding and for landscape use. Phlox Salmon Glow in bloom in the background

CHAPTER IV

CULTURE

Garden culture of the chrysanthemum can be about the last word in simplicity. Again, it offers possibilities in intensity of culture that are extremely interesting.

Almost every locality has its groups or borders of old-fashioned kinds, many years established, receiving little or no attention. Yet they flourish—perhaps not exactly like the proverbial bay tree, but flowering year after year nevertheless. The colors are apt to be indefinite and somewhat rusty but still acceptable and desirable in their place.

These neglected but persistent plantings indicate rather emphatically that the chrysanthemum is far from fussy as to growing conditions. There is a vast difference, however, between this type and that which receives good culture. No other garden plant responds more quickly or liberally to good treatment. No other garden group is so useful or necessary in rounding out the garden season. No gardener, then, will deny them the good care they deserve.

Occasionally the objection is brought forth that the chrysanthemum occupies garden space for a long period that could be used to better advantage. Perhaps this argument was reasonable when only the old-fashioned late-blooming varieties were available. But it no longer holds, for two very definite reasons. First, several of the more recent kinds are in full flower as early as August. Second, if space is at a premium in the show garden, why devote that space to the chrysanthemum throughout the season? Chrysanthemums transplant so readily in late August and September, with no impairment to their later flowering, that it is good garden practice to follow up summer-flowering annuals and also to fill out conspicuous vacancies in the hardy border with plants that have been grown during summer in the service or vegetable garden or in any out-of-the-way area.

GARDENING INTENSIVELY

A practical example of intensive gardening is brought to mind; it happens to concern a prominently located formal garden. Here a fine spring display of narcissi, Darwin and Breeder Tulips, and other bulbs is followed by bedding plants, such as heliotrope, snapdragon, and other favorite annuals. In September, when frost injury usually occurs, these tender plants are promptly replaced with chrysanthemums that have been grown in rows in the vegetable garden. Lifted with a ball of soil, although buds have formed (some even showing color), and planted carefully, no check or injury occurs. Thus a gorgeous display is assured, often extending well into November. Surplus plants left in the vegetable garden provide an abundance of good cut-flower material, so that there is no need for cutting from the garden proper.

Tulips and other spring-flowering bulbs are planted in late November, after the chrysanthemums have been taken up, heeled in (planted closely) in a sheltered spot, and given a light covering for winter. The following May they are taken up, divided, planted out in rows, and held in readiness again for late-summer replacements.

Plants for flowering indoors can also be potted or tubbed as they come into bud. By using late-flowering varieties, the season can be extended to Thanksgiving, or even later. After they have provided this windfall of late beauty, they can be heeled in in a frame or some sheltered spot for spring division and replanting.

CONDENSED RULES OF CULTURE

The more important needs of the garden chrysanthemum, summed up briefly, are enumerated here for quick reference. (See also Culture in Detail, page 68.)

HARDY CHRYSANTHEMUMS

Location

Plants should not be shaded more than one third of the day; should not be wind-swept from north or east; should be reasonably well drained.

Soil

Good average soil, such as required by any vegetable crop.

Fertilizer

Well-rotted cow or barnyard manure, plus 20 per cent superphosphate; leafmold or peat moss, supplemented by a balanced chemical fertilizer.

Soil Preparation

Deep rooting is important. Soil should be prepared to a depth of 15 to 18 inches, incorporating all fertilizers thoroughly. This assures healthy plants that can better resist insects and diseases.

Time to Plant

Spring planting is safest.

Type of Plant

Avoid old, overgrown clumps. Healthy divisions or pieces taken from an old plant or healthy young growing pot plants give best results.

CULTURE

Spacing of Plants

Do not crowd! This induces more trouble than all other causes. Eighteen inches apart or 18 inches from any other plant is close enough.

Pruning or Pinching

To avoid lanky or spindly plant growth, pinch the plants at intervals from spring until late July, removing 1 inch of top growth first when shoots are 6 to 9 inches high, continuing at intervals. Never pinch or prune back to hard, brittle wood.

Summer Feeding

Under no conditions apply chemical fertilizers when the soil is dry. They may burn the foliage. Occasional applications of fertilizers during the summer are desirable but can be injurious. (Refer to page 79 for details.)

Spraying

Use fresh Bordeaux mixture for foliage diseases; Black Leaf 40 or nicotine in some form (always with soap), for sucking insects such as aphis; for caterpillars and other eating insects, lead arsenate or a good pyrethrum insecticide. Never use soap with Bordeaux, arsenate of lead, or any spray containing lime; foliage burning may ensue. Burning may also occur if insecticides are applied immediately after several cloudy days; also from spraying in strong sunshine. Early or late in the day is safer.

Staking

Seldom necessary if plants are pinched as suggested. Tall-growing kinds can be staked when buds first set. Stakes should be substantial but should not exceed the height of plant at this time. The trunk or main stem only should be tied, using heavy soft cord. Never tie in the entire plant; the effect is heavy and unnatural.

CULTURE IN DETAIL

Planting Time

Spring is the best time to plant. Inasmuch as the plants have until autumn to build up flowering wood, the planting period may extend later than would be advisable for the average hardy perennial. In New England small, healthy plants set out as late as July will flower freely by October. Best results are obtained, however, when plants have become established and are making good root and top growth before hot weather sets in. This means planting not later than May or early June—proportionately earlier in Southern latitudes.

Dividing Old Plants

Plants that have been carried over in the garden should be divided in spring; moderate-growing kinds every second year, and the vigorous, heavy-stooling kinds every year. This is best done shortly after the spring growth appears, when the tops of the stolons or suckers begin to leaf out and have developed some new roots. Divisions from the outer part of the clump are strongest. Those with two or three "leads" or new shoots will make large plants by autumn. Small single divisions, carrying a few roots, with careful culture will also make good plants. The core or central part of the old clump is not apt to produce a healthy, vigorous growth, so should not be used.

Purchasing Plants

In purchasing stock, young, healthy, growing plants from 2½- or 3-inch pots are safest. This is particularly true when they are secured and shipped from a distance. Field roots are fragile at best and apt to suffer in transit; also they should be planted reasonably early in spring. Plants from pots can be planted safely about a month after spring gets under way. In New England the planting season extends up until the time roses are in bloom, or from early May until early July. Occasionally a severe late frost may nip newly set pot plants, but this seldom is very injurious because within two weeks or so new growths appear from the base of the plant. As a matter of fact, a more branching, huskier plant is apt to be the result of such a frost nip.

Distance to Plant

Varieties differ much in habit of growth; growing conditions also vary greatly. Therefore, it is impossible to be absolutely specific as to planting distances. Moderate-growing kinds, such as Normandie, Early Bronze Pompon, and those of erect habit, such as Orion and Aladdin, can be spaced from 12 to 15 inches apart. Average-growing kinds, such as Ruth Hatton, Jean Treadway, Diana, and Ethel, should be planted 18 inches apart. Vigorous-branching kinds, including most of the Single Korean Hybrids, are spaced 22 to 24 inches apart.

The above distances apply to solid beds, keeping the plants at least half of this distance from the edge or border. If planted in rows for cutting purposes or for later transplanting (but with convenience in cultivation chiefly in mind), 24 inches between rows may be allowed for those specified 18 inches apart and 36 inches for those recommended for 24 inches apart. With good culture this spacing will just barely permit reasonable walking room when the plants are in flower.

Planting in the Border

In the mixed border chrysanthemums appear to excellent advantage. They do much to prolong interest in the garden for several weeks, whether planted in spring or used to fill in the occasional hiatus that usually occurs in late summer, even in the best of gardens. Individual plants can be distributed to spread color effectively, but groups of three or four of one color are more striking. However planted, sufficient space should be allowed for healthy development at all times. Crowding among annuals and other plants is one of the surest ways to encourage foliage diseases, red spider, and other insect pests.

Location

A fallacy that still prevails to a considerable extent is that the chrysanthemum should have some immediate shelter, such as a wall or background. This was true years ago, when only late-flowering kinds were available, and it is still true so far as this type of mum is concerned. For earlier varieties an open location where sunshine is available two thirds of the day; where there is freedom from the competition of tree roots; and where there is good air circulation, such as exists in the average garden, is all that is needed. A badly wind-swept or drafty exposure is, of course, undesirable, because the cold, biting winds and first real killing frost will be most damaging under these conditions, injuring the chrysanthemums sometimes two or three weeks before their season should really end. Such cold exposures, however, seldom exist in the average garden. As a matter of fact, commercial growers grow chrysanthemums in the open field, subject to exposure and all weather conditions, with very satisfactory results. The important point is to choose kinds that are early enough to assure a good display during your chrysanthemum season.

Drainage

Chrysanthemums, like the majority of plants, dislike wet feet during winter. Most winterkilling occurs in soils where water stands or settles around the crown during the occasional winter thaws. A reasonably well-drained situation, such as exists in the average garden, is needed. If there is a question on this point, however, it will be safer to take up the plants after flowering and heel them in under the protection of a cold frame or in a sheltered spot that has good drainage.

Soil and Its Preparation

Soil that will grow satisfactory vegetables and other garden plants will grow good chrysanthemums; whether it is alkaline or acid (within a reasonable range) seems to make little difference. Wonderfully fine chrysanthemums have been produced in heavy soil in which sufficient lime had been used to show a considerable alkaline reaction. Equally good plants in a light soil of a peaty nature —and of course acid—are often observed. This indicates that careful attention to summer culture is the really important essential. The chrysanthemum is a gross feeder and can stand extremely heavy fertilizing. Overfed plants, however, do not well resist early frosts, because the petal substance is lacking. Their roots also overwinter poorly. Scrubby or half-starved plants are lacking in vitality and are, therefore, equally susceptible. Good culture is the happy medium.

"Tilth" is recognized by the European gardener as being fundamental to good garden growth. Tilth means the thorough mellowing or breaking up of the soil so that it will absorb moisture and heat and will aerate properly as deep or deeper than the roots will penetrate. Good tilth is important to any worth-while plant but particularly so to the chrysanthemum because it induces deep rooting. Plants well furnished underneath are not punished by surface heating and drying; consequently, they better resist the long, dry, hot spells that are likely to occur. By the same token, they are better equipped to survive severe winter conditions.

It is well, then, to prepare the soil to a depth of 15 to 18 inches, or even somewhat deeper. If the soil is naturally lean or poor, manure it liberally, using well-decayed cow manure if available. Prepared or shredded cow, sheep, or poultry manure would be the next choice, in the order named, and can usually be obtained readily through seedsman, florist, or local nurseryman. Phosphate is highly desirable and can be added with the manure in the form of bone meal or superphosphate. My preference is 20 per cent superphosphate, which can be spread as heavily as 1 pound to twenty-five square feet. (This works out, roughly, to about a good handful per plant.) This, with the manure, should be worked thoroughly into and through the soil, to a depth of 12 or 15 inches. The addition of peat is desirable in soils that are light and sandy, or the opposite— too sticky and clayey. Leafmold will serve the same purpose, but the chrysanthemum appears to be particularly fond of the imported granulated peat.

With such thorough preparation to begin with, it will be a simple matter to supply additional feeding any time during summer that its need is indicated. This deep, thorough preparation will, of course, leave the soil in a soft and spongy condition. All plants require a reasonably firm soil for proper root development; therefore, the soil should be firmed by rolling or gently treading before planting.

Planting

The proper setting of plants is a simple operation, but it is surprising how often one finds instances where plants are merely put into the ground —not *planted*. The soil should be reasonably firmed, neither packed hard nor left too soft. In firming the soil around the roots—and here it should be *well* firmed—the pressure is needed mostly at the root tips, not at the crown of the plant. In setting field plants or clumps, the roots should be spread out to a depth of 3 or 4 inches. The soil immediately covering these roots should be firmed, as well as that around the plant proper. When finished, the crown should be not more than 1 inch below the surface or bed level. Smaller divisions are set so that an inch or two of the tip shows above the ground. If the roots are long, they can be laid in at an angle, not more than 4 inches deep at the lower extreme. Pot plants should be set with the upper surface of the ball of soil about 2 inches below the surface level.

Water can be applied best if a saucer-shaped depression, large enough to hold a quart or two, is formed around each plant as it is set. This is filled with water at least twice. When the water has been absorbed, the soil is leveled in, leaving the surface soil loose. A day or two after planting, check your plants for firmness. If a light pull will dislodge one, it is evidence that it was not sufficiently well firmed.

SUMMER CARE

Cultivation

Well-cared-for plants will go through the season without suffering any real check in growing. They are, of course, better able to resist the minor ailments that invariably affect weak or stunted plants. Good culture, then, should be given during the growing season. Persistent cultivation—which means keeping the surface soil loose and free at all times—is first in importance. Next is proper watering at the right time. A healthy, vigorous-growing plant is attractive in itself long before it reaches the flowering stage. It has definite accent or group value in the garden and, therefore, justifies every bit of attention necessary to give it vigorous, robust growth.

Pinching

This term—entirely familiar in commercial circles, as applied to plants—is often confusing or meaningless to the amateur. It means pinching about 2 inches of growth from the tips of the main shoots, so that they will produce many more side or lateral branches rather than a few tall, ungainly growths. The term is derived from the fact that the soft tip growth is *pinched* out with the finger and thumb, which is the easiest and best way to take care of this important detail—best, because the beginner is apt to prune too low, where the wood is beginning to harden. Severe pruning has a tendency to set back or cripple the plant to the extent that it will not produce healthy side growths; therefore, whether you use the finger-and-thumb method or shears, keep close to the tips, where the growth is soft.

As pointed out previously, too many main shoots, or growths coming from the base of the plant, make an overabundance of wood that is apt to become dry and brittle by midsummer. The plant is literally overloaded with growth that has stretched too far away from the root system to get a full supply of the sap that is so needed for late growth. Start your plants, then, with not more than three of these shoots. Even one will make a fine plant in all but the weakest-growing kinds. When this growth is 6 inches high, nip off an inch or so from the tip. This will force the quick development of several side branches. Some of these side branches will likely be stronger than the others and soon assume an ascending habit. When these are about 9 inches long, again pinch off the tips. Continue this process at intervals until a bushy plant is formed.

In New England this pinching may be continued, except with the very early varieties, until late July. In this way a low, branchy plant, with nothing but soft, vigorous wood, will have developed (see illustration). It should be a lusty, healthy specimen and an ornament long before it flowers—lusty, because the plump stems carry the food elements, in sap form, freely through the plant, and also because the healthy, fully developed leaves get their share of moisture, and doubtless some food elements, from the night air. There is no "hardening of the arteries," none of the constriction so common to the overgrown undivided plant. Seldom will staking be required, and, last but not least, the sprays when cut will take up water readily, enabling them to keep fresh for days longer.

Watering

Knowing when and how to water are really somewhat of a horticultural accomplishment. Even in the larger greenhouse establishments, where growing conditions are under perfect control, where men are specially trained in the various branches, it is still difficult to find one who can water properly. He who has developed the necessary instinct is indeed in the *rara avis* class. It is not to be expected, then, that the average person can immediately master this cultural detail. The whole secret is not to water until needed and then to water *copiously*.

As with roses and other plants that are spaced some distance apart, watering the plants individually is best. Chrysanthemums differ from the average garden plant, however, in that they develop a rapid top growth in late summer and a heavy mat of extremely fibrous roots. During prolonged dry spells all moisture under the roots may became entirely exhausted. More than an ordinary rain is required to penetrate to this depth, and one can readily be deceived into assuming all is well just because the surface soil seems moist. It is better, when in doubt, to investigate by troweling out a soil sample to a depth of 8 or 9 inches. In doing so, don't be deceived by the darker color of the soil at this depth. If it crumbles easily and has a dry feel, then water freely. Slight wilting of the tips during

HEALTHY, well-grown plants. These were set out, from
3-inch pots, in June, following Darwin tulips. The spacing
—15 inches apart—is almost too close. *Photographed in
August.*

THE EFFECT of overcrowding. Too much competition—
due to lack of division and neglect in pinching—accounts
for weak-stemmed, scraggy plants of this sort, sure to lop
over in the first storm.

the heat of the day usually indicates a dry soil condition.

A chrysanthemum in full growth needs a lot of water. The best way to apply this is to open a furrow or saucer completely around the plant, just beyond the root line. No harm is done if a few roots are exposed. The saucer or trench should be deep enough to hold at least ½ gallon of water. It should be filled two, three, or more times, until the water is absorbed but slowly. Level in the soil the following day, and you will have the satisfaction of knowing that in addition to a thorough watering a good job of cultivating is accomplished at the same time. Lest you get the impression that this is too laborious, let me assure you that three such waterings are sufficient for the driest of New England summers and really much less troublesome than frequently sprinkling the entire bed, which invariably necessitates immediate aftercultivation to prevent baking.

Summer Feeding

It is not good practice to force growth unduly during early summer, but plants that are stunted or fail to grow satisfactorily may be jolted out of this condition by an application of nitrate of soda or nitrogen in some other readily absorbable form. Liquid manure is safe at any time and is readily prepared by diluting ½ to 1 bushel of cow manure —which need not be decomposed. Tie it loosely in an ordinary burlap bag and place this in a cask or half barrel where it can be allowed to soak overnight; then stir and add water until a mild coffee color is obtained. Where quick results are desired, nitrate of soda can be dissolved, a heaping teaspoonful per gallon, in the solution.

Usually by late August or early September a stimulant of some sort will be in order. Complete commercial fertilizers, such as Vigoro or Loma, or nitrates in the form of nitrate of soda, sulfate of ammonia, or calcium nitrate can be used. An excellent way to apply any of these fertilizers is to add it to the last application of water when the plants are being watered as suggested above. Two or 3 tablespoonfuls per plant, depending upon the type of fertilizer, is sufficient. (Manufacturer's directions should be followed carefully.)

If fertilizer is spread on the soil surface, care should be taken not to apply it too close to the plant stem. The active, or feeding, roots begin 9 inches or more from the center, and the fertilizer is spread beyond this. Again, it can be emphasized that chemical or prepared fertilizers should never be used when the soil is in a dry condition. That is what usually causes injury, rather than the fertilizer alone. As a matter of fact, fertilizers that would not cause burning under such conditions would be of dubious value. Water your plants thoroughly, then, before fertilizing; and be sure, of course, that no fertilizer remains on the foliage.

In connection with soil conditions and fertilizers,

it occasionally happens that no amount of manuring or fertilizing is effective. This may be due to a completely worn-out condition of the soil or to the absence or overabundance of some one food element. Agricultural chemists have perfected soil testing to the point where a very accurate analysis can be made. The majority of the state agricultural experiment stations are equipped to make this analysis and do so, without charge, as a service to the public. The gardener who has soil difficulties will find that an occasional checkup is real economy, aside from its other advantages. There is a tremendous amount of money spent each year on fertilizers that do not fertilize, and such waste is by no means always the fault of the brand that is used. Write your experiment station for directions in taking soil samples, stating in a general way what the soil is being used for. This should be done some two or three weeks before planting time.

Staking

Lanky-growing plants are a source of grief to the gardener. Usually when this condition is first noticed, it is too late properly to correct it. It is difficult to make branches that once have looped over assume an erect position and still look perfectly natural. Judicious staking will help, however. Use a substantial stake, ½ to 1 inch through, drive firmly into the ground as near to the center of the plant as possible, and tie it firmly with heavy, soft twine to the trunk or main branches. Two or three stakes may be required for a heavy plant. This staking should be done not later than August. The stakes should be no higher than the top of the plant at this time, so that the additional growth to come will soon entirely conceal the stake.

Spraying

In some localities good chrysanthemums grow year after year with never a spraying. Unfortunately these exceptions are becoming less frequent as the "garden urge" progresses. The average well-groomed garden, with its ever-increasing diversity of plant material, is frequented by various insects. While these pests seldom seriously injure chrysanthemums, it is desirable to spray occasionally in the interest of better foliage and flowers.

None of the spray mixtures ordinarily used on other garden material will injure the chrysanthemum, and they at least serve as a repellent or preventive. Give the mums a "shot," too, then, whenever spraying operations are under way. If your roses are due for a Tri-ogen bath, include the chrysanthemums in your schedule. It will tone up the foliage and discourage possible insect or blight attacks. A good pump is absolutely essential. To be effective, the spray material should strike the plants in a mist-like vapor that reaches all parts. Such a spray depends upon good air pressure—something that makeshift equipment will not produce. Inas-

ABOVE, large plants, in full bud, being moved in from the service garden. Soil is tamped down firmly about the roots. Below, to prevent wilting they are given a copious watering. Soil should be leveled in the following day. And then —(*see illustration facing page 83*).

THREE WEEKS after being moved, a riot of color despite severe frosts.

much as an excellent small pressure pump can be had at reasonable cost, it should be regarded as an essential investment. Continued wet foliage is conducive to blight or fungous diseases, also certain insect pests (see Nematodes). For that reason the practice of spraying with clear water is now being discontinued, even in greenhouse culture.

WINTER PROTECTION

Overkindness in the form of too much covering is undoubtedly responsible for more winterkilling than any amount of freezing. It will be noted that there is usually a greater loss in a mild winter, largely because the covering material is apt to smother the crown of the plant and cause decay. No one can forecast the coming winter successfully; in New England even the "seers of the caterpillar" fail dismally, so the best we can do is to assume that it will be about average—and cover accordingly. Where hardy plants are concerned, we can be governed by the premise that the best any winter covering can do is to keep cold *in* the ground rather than *out* of it. In other words, it may help to maintain an even condition that lessens the possibility of alternate freezing and thawing, which are the real causes of nearly all winterkilling.

Covering materials, accordingly, should not be put on too soon. Let the plants mature properly and get hardened by a good frost. Before covering, cut the tops back to within 5 or 6 inches of the crown.

The remaining stubs will help hold the covering materials in place. Then apply a light covering, which can be added to after additional freezing penetrates the soil to a depth of several inches. Such gradual covering is better than putting it all on at once.

Covering Material

Hemlock or spruce branches, if they can be secured, make ideal winter covering. They should be laid flat so that they screen the soil sufficiently to act as a barrier to the wind and action of the sun. A sprinkling of leaves or short straw may be added to fill possible gaps between branches. Salt hay is the best material for this purpose. It is weedless, clings to the ground well, and can be carried over for use a second season. Usually it can be secured from your local nurseryman, feed store, or farmer's co-operative in bales running about 150 pounds in weight. It should be shaken out very thoroughly and then applied loosely to a depth of 3 or 4 inches. This will settle down to an inch or so by spring and is sufficient. There is seldom difficulty in keeping it in place, but in exposed locations it may be weighted down with branches or boards. One bale of salt hay is sufficient to cover the average garden.

Leaves

As Nature applies them, leaves make a splendid blanket. They sift down gradually and form a cushion that is never too heavy. When mere man applies them, they are almost sure to mat and with every thaw become a soggy, smothering mass. Leaves can, however, be used satisfactorily, providing some roughage is first used directly around the crown of the plant. This may be branches or coarse stalks from the garden. Chrysanthemum tops can be used, providing they are from healthy plants. But it is better to destroy the tops entirely if there was any suspicion of foliage disease the previous season or if the corn borer is included among the local pests. Above all, do not get impatient or too concerned about the coming of winter and cover too early. Remember that the plants are still making soft growth from the crowns so long as there is warmth in the soil, and this growth the covering is apt to destroy. By the same token, do not uncover too early in the spring. That first warm day, when frost is leaving the ground and spring is in the air, is usually a snare and a delusion, but the impulse to uncover one's winter-bound plants is strong. Better play safe, and uncover gradually rather than all at once.

LIFTING PLANTS OVER WINTER

Try this out in an experimental way if your mums persistently winterkill regardless of covering. Just before winter dig a few plants, retaining a fairly good ball of soil around the roots. Locate a sheltered corner in the garden where rain or snow water will not settle. Stand the plants close together right on top of the ground, working leaves or strawy manure between and around the roots, lightly covering the crowns. Since the area required will be small, it will be an easy matter to raise the elevation if needed to insure drainage. This method has worked out remarkably well under the changeable conditions of Connecticut, indicating again that seldom is freezing the cause of winterkilling, but that the soggy, wet condition around the plant crowns following temporary thaws is responsible. This method has proven altogether satisfactory over three winters. While this is not sufficient to establish it as a general practice, it does indicate that this method is well worth a trial.

CHRYSANTHEMUMS AS CUT FLOWERS

Few flowers have the fine keeping qualities and the diversity of type, color, and variety found in the mum family. Unquestionably the Single types lend themselves better to cut-flower arrangement than do the Double types. Although the Pompons have perhaps better keeping qualities, the Korean Hybrids are particularly lovely and adaptable for dainty arrangements. If properly grown, there will be no difficulty so far as keeping qualities go—three to four weeks for cut sprays is not unusual. Where culture has been faulty, thus causing the stems to be brittle and constricted, water is not taken up in sufficient quantity. Then the only recourse is to shorten the stem by snapping off an inch or so every day or two.

CULTURE

Various artificial aids are suggested from time to time, such as aspirin or the use of copper containers. Their value is questionable but some special cut-flower preservatives have merit. Occasionally large chrysanthemums purchased from a florist will wilt hopelessly in a few hours. If so, it should not be assumed that it is because they are overripe or stale; by and large florists are particular on that point. Grown in cool greenhouses and kept so in the florist shop, the change to a heated, often drafty apartment is too abrupt.

When receiving these large florist flowers it is a good idea to break off—not cut—2 or 3 inches from the stems. Use fresh water and a sufficiently large and deep container. Keep them in a cool place on the floor for a few hours or overnight; thus they will harden and take up the needed moisture. Badly wilted flowers can often be revived by this treatment, but I would suggest lukewarm or tepid water and the addition of 1 teaspoonful of salt to each quart. (Try this also on Oriental Poppies. It is simpler than hot-water treatment or searing the ends of stems.)

Chrysanthemums can be cut in the garden any time during the day. Strip the foliage so that no leaves get in the water, breaking off the stem ends; place in a cool, draft-free spot overnight. Change the water every second day; snap off an inch or so of the stem; then rinse, and you will be delighted with their long-keeping qualities.

HARDY CHRYSANTHEMUMS

GARDEN CHRYSANTHEMUMS IN THE SOUTH
AND SOUTHWEST

By nature a cool-weather subject, the chrysanthemum is never exactly happy under the warmer conditions of the South and Southwest. Nevertheless, rather surprising results can develop with special treatment.

The South has an advantage in that nearly all of the greenhouse sorts can be carried over the winter or dormant season without great difficulty. I have seen sample flowers grown in Louisiana which compared very favorably with the Northern greenhouse product. Undoubtedly the location near the Gulf of Mexico was a factor. Further inland, with conditions more arid, mums can be grown successfully. I have had excellent reports concerning the Korean Hybrids and other typically hardy types from growers in St. Louis, Missouri; Rome, Georgia, and Texas, where extreme summer heat prevails.

Here is the method used by my brother, who grew to perfection the Korean Hybrids in Rome, Georgia, when they were first introduced. It should apply to any of the garden kinds. In each instance the first and most important requirement seems water—lots of water. Next, get the young plants in the ground as early as possible so that a good lively root system will be built up while the soil is reasonably cool. Plant early; then as the dry season approaches outline the beds with a 6-inch board edging tight enough to hold water. Flood the beds when water is needed, which might be every day during very hot, dry periods. Never water overhead or sprinkle in such a way that the foliage becomes wet. (See page 110.)

This persistent flooding treatment, while it does supply the needed amount of water, unfortunately also leaches the soil and has a tendency to bring the roots to the surface, leaving the plant with little winter resistance. A light top-dressing of a good compost, applied at intervals during summer, and finished off with a 3-inch mulch (one half good soil, one half decayed manure), applied when the plants were in full flower, corrected this. In fact, the problem under these conditions is not the winter loss of plants, but how to use to advantage the multitude of healthy young plants that are produced. Here again the importance of dividing the old plants as early in spring as possible is stressed.

Conditions through the vast Southland and the Midwest are so varied that it would be imprudent to recommend any specific treatment.

EXHIBITION CHRYSANTHEMUMS IN THE GARDEN

Those large mums so conspicuous at the autumn flower shows and in the flower shops from October right up to New Year's can be grown in the garden if one selects the earlier kinds, and if the garden season extends well into November. Gardens in some parts of New England adjacent to the seashore and in areas around New York are favorable for outdoor culture of such large florists' varieties. From Philadelphia south, except in high altitudes, they can be grown quite generally.

The growing of these larger types, however, involves considerable cultural skill and a lot of close attention at all times.

In addition to the true "exhibition" chrysanthemums (those large ball-shaped blooms) we can include here the Single type, some of which, when disbudded, are decidedly effective for arrangements, or as pot plants. The Anemone type and the Pompons also respond to disbudding.

To produce those big flowers, start just as early as your season will permit, with healthy young plants. To begin with, all that you will need will be one succulent shoot or rooted cutting. This will be the foundation of your entire plant. When this shoot has grown to a height of 7 to 9 inches, pinch off or cut away about 2 inches of the tip, which should include one or two well-developed leaves. Soon several lateral growths will appear.

Now decide just how many flowers you want this plant to produce. If the largest flower possible is your aim, then two shoots to a plant would be right; some growers prefer just one. The majority of kinds, however, will produce up to three flowers per plant without any significant loss in size. Leaving three shoots gives the grower a little leeway, too, in the event that one or two of the branches may be

PINK SPOON, a variety popular for cutting, especially for arrangements, was developed by Eugene H. Michel.

PALE MOON, with medium-sized flowers in large sprays,
is a lovely soft color; choice for cutting. Early October.

accidentally broken. If the decision is to be three, then remove all but three of the new shoots, which are then grown on without interruption through the season.

Additional side shoots will appear from time to time and should be promptly removed. As autumn approaches, the first flower bud will appear. Later, additional flower buds in clusters. Now disbudding begins. This means the removal of *all but one bud*, usually the tip or crown bud, although some growers choose ("take" is the grower's term—it actually means "leave") one of the secondary or terminal buds, because in certain varieties these terminal buds make more perfect blooms. The development of these buds, until they reach perfection in the finished flower, is the test of the grower's skill.

For cut-flower purposes, however, or decoration in the home, size should be a second consideration. Flowers of average size may be used for so many purposes, and they keep better. A plant well finished, whatever the type, can produce ten to twelve very acceptable blooms. Whatever the number, keep in mind that each shoot will require a stake, and too many stakes in the garden can be objectionable. This staking begins when the shoots are about a foot high. Stakes are changed as needed, the final stake reaching up close to the flower. Bamboo stakes are usually employed, and should be strong enough to support the shoot, but, for appearance's sake, as light as is practical.

91

Attention to other cultural details is important. The plant must be kept growing without check of any kind or a woody or "bony" stem will develop. Soil that is too dry, well down under the plant where the feeding roots are, is the usual cause. Commercial fertilizer improperly applied is likely to be next in order.

Spray consistently for insects, but particularly after the bud appears; aphis and leaf hoppers can do serious injury at this stage. The finished flower will be at its very best about the time frost, or at least bad weather, can be expected. Those big open blooms are sensitive, so some form of shelter must be provided.

This is difficult in the garden. A cold frame or bed over which a temporary skeleton structure can be put up is the most practical. It should be strong enough to support cold-frame sash or well-made cellophane sash. Side protection should be provided in the form of canvas or "black cloth" (such as florists use) when cold winds and frosts come, and so arranged that it can be taken down quickly when not needed. Most of this equipment can be stored for another season. There is use, of course, for cold-frame and other sash all through the season, so the investment will be justified.

EXHIBITION BLOOMS IN POTS

There are definite advantages in growing the big fellows in pots, chief of which is that they can be shifted around during the season and finally brought indoors to finish off. Later-blooming varieties can be grown and the season accordingly prolonged. Here again the cold frame is in order because protection from overabundant or driving rains can be provided. Start with cuttings or young plants from 2½-inch pots in spring when danger from heavy frost is past—early May here in the East; earlier as one goes South. Pinching and disbudding (as previously described) will be in order, as will the number of stems allowed to each plant, but with this difference—a single-stem plant developing just one flower makes possible the acme of size and perfection. In a pot the growth can be better controlled, while in the garden the height of a plant with but one flower would likely make it awkward and out of proportion to everything in sight.

For soil for the pots use a good basic compost. This will answer for each potting operation, so provide enough for the entire season. Top soil such as is found in the average garden, with the addition of properly balanced fertilizers, will grow exhibition-caliber chrysanthemums. The ideal would be a rather heavy field soil, 50 per cent of which would be turfy. The turfs should be laid up a year in advance, grass side down, built up in layers of 1 foot, then a 4-inch layer of good cow manure. In other words, the proportion would be one part manure to four parts soil. This will break down over winter and be friable enough for easy potting. Some fibrous grass roots will remain in the compost, but they are beneficial, and the best source of humus. Bone meal, phosphate, or other fertilizers can be added as needed when potting operations take place.

Repotting should be taken care of as needed; that is, as the pots become well filled with roots, *but before they become pot bound.* As larger pots are used, it is important to pot firmly, using a stick—something about lath width—for a tamp. Care must be taken, too, not to disturb the ball of soil in the process. Reasonable firmness is what is needed. This tamping can be overdone. A common mistake, also, lies in the temptation to shift into too large pots. A good ratio would be from 2½ or 3-inch to 4-inch; from 4 to 6-inch; with an additional shift to 8-inch if needed. Drainage must be provided in the larger-size pots, say from 5 inches up. A piece of broken pot large enough to cover the hole should be laid in first, curved side up, and covered with ½ inch or more of small pieces of broken pots, screened cinders, or broken charcoal.

At the time the last shift is made, additional enrichment can be added to the compost. The old-time grower swore by bone or horn shavings, with a preference for the latter. Clay's fertilizer used as a top-dressing was also a favorite, with Scotch soot as an alternate. These are difficult to secure at present, but bone meal, horn dust, and dried blood are available and will prove altogether satisfactory. Any of the good brands of well-balanced commercial fertilizer can be used for top-dressing.

Applications of liquid manure, plus a teaspoonful of nitrate of soda per gallon stirred in, can be used, when root growth is well established, up until the blossom begins to show color; then feeding should be discontinued. However, where plants are badly pot bound when in bloom, a weekly application of mild liquid manure will help.

There is no "rule of thumb" to cover feeding. Much depends on the soil to begin with. Watch the foliage. It should show a rich green and have a lusty appearance, but be not too brittle, which is a sign of excessive feeding. If the foliage is light green, soft, and somewhat limp in texture, feeding is indicated, providing excessive watering, poor drainage, or overpotting are not contributing causes. The grower acquires a sixth sense with experience. Careful observation is the watchword.

WATERING

This is the most important detail of all. Without proper watering, feeding can be positively injurious. A sick plant is susceptible to every insect and disease. Take particular care with watering. It will simplify matters if the pots are plunged up to the rim in soil, spaced far enough apart so the foliage barely touches. In repotting, leave sufficient room for water above the soil in the pot—½ inch for small pots, a full inch for the larger sizes. Plants plunged in the open ground can become water-logged, either from overwatering or from excessive rains. This causes the foliage to wilt. To correct this, take up the pot and lay the plant over on its side until the soil appears dry. Check the drainage before returning to its place, when careful watering can be resumed.

The specialist who grows pot mums for exhibition can usually tell at a glance which plant requires water, but not always, particularly where the pots are very large. Damp atmospheric conditions may give the soil a moist appearance and keep the foliage spruced up, yet the roots may be actually suffering from lack of moisture. Since this same condition causes many a house plant to go wrong in the dead of winter, it may be well to master the one infallible method of knowing when to water, when not to water; namely, rap the rim of the pot with your knuckle. A dull, dead sound means sufficient moisture; a ringing, resonant sound means that water is needed. Practice this method for a short time and you will find the watering problem will be no problem at all.

OVERWINTERING GREENHOUSE AND NOT-TOO-HARDY CHRYSANTHEMUMS

Here again the cold frame proves its usefulness. For overwintering chrysanthemums, the frame should be somewhat countersunk—a foot or more below ground level. Pot plants after flowering can be trimmed down and the pots plunged in the soil right to the top of the rim; or the plants can be knocked out and plunged close together. This may save pot breakage. Garden varieties a little on the tender side can also be heeled in, plant to plant, with the crowns barely exposed. A light covering of leaves or strawy material will be all that is needed. The frame should be reasonably tight and heavily shaded sash used. The important consideration is to keep moisture out of the frame. Plants should be watered, of course, when put in the frame; from then on kept rather on the dry side. Some ventilation will be needed throughout the winter as warm days occur. Then give plenty of ventilation during the warm days of early spring to keep the new growth firm and healthy so that a good supply of cuttings will be available for the season's new crop.

PROPAGATING EXHIBITION CHRYSANTHEMUMS

Cuttings can be rooted in sand (as described on page 134), but for this purpose simply take the young 3- to 4-inch growths with a rather hard heel or base, pot them firmly in 2½-inch pots, using a mixture of light soil and sand in equal parts. No fertilizer of any kind at this stage. Water well; then plunge the pots in the frame; shade the cuttings from the sun. Keep the frame fairly close and draft free until roots and some new growth appear. Care must be taken not to overwater at this stage.

SHADE-CLOTH (BLACK) CULTURE

Since it was discovered that light, or rather absence of light, to a large extent governs the blooming season of chrysanthemums, commercial growers have hastened the flowering season two months or more, successfully flowering in September kinds that normally flower in mid-October. Blooms can be obtained earlier or later, as desired, simply by timing the application of black cloth. This method will prove distinctly useful to gardeners in those areas where the season is too short for garden mums. Hotels, suburban eating places, and the many public institutions using cut flowers in quantity can, without too much trouble, provide a good supply for September when other garden material is not too plentiful.

In practice, the plants are completely covered some time before dark with black sateen cloth which remains over them until about 7 A.M., thus, in effect, putting them to bed early and making them sleep late. For this particular type of culture plants, of course, should be started early so a good growth will be made before the shade cloth is applied; the plants to be pinched at least once to assure best production.

The proper procedure can be arrived at by deciding first the desired flowering date. Let us assume this to be September, which would be about a month before the real chrysanthemum time in the

Growing florists' varieties of chrysanthemums, outdoors under cloth shading, makes an interesting hobby for the amateur. Disbudded and trained to single stems, they produce blooms rivaling the finest greenhouse specimens.

IN OUTDOOR CULTURE of florists' varieties, protection from wind and frost, and artificial darkness to hasten flowering, are provided by shading cloth supported on

garden. As an example, take the pink Pompon Jewell, normally flowering in the garden about October 15. Working backward, to bring Jewell into flower about September 5, shading should commence about sixty days previous, or July 5; the plants should have been pinched not later than June 7, and planted in the frame by May 15—if earlier, so much the better.

Roughly, then, planting should be done at least six weeks before shading commences, then allow two months of shade-cloth application to bring the plants into color. There will, of course, be a slight time variation if earlier or later flowering dates are used; again, different varieties require a longer or shorter period of shading. It is well to choose kinds that flower normally about the same date and good practice to avoid very late kinds. Use a good quality cloth, a grade specifying a light intensity of 2-foot candles or less. Your supply house can secure this cloth for you from the manufacturer. The equipment indicated under cold-frame culture (page 109) will serve, except that the black cloth is used to cover the frame completely.

The following detailed discussion of growing hardy mums under cloth has been prepared for this volume by Mr. George L. Blake, an expert in this particular field.

The chrysanthemum enthusiast who enjoys the wealth of rare beauty and color his garden displays when everything else has ceased to bloom can find added enjoyment and pleasure in setting out a bed of exhibition-sized mums, provided he is willing to take on a little extra work and invest in a frame and frost tent to protect them in mid-October and through a good part of November. Where a bit of friendly rivalry between neighbors can be developed, there is, indeed, opportunity for displays which many consider hardly possible in the latitude of New York and farther North.

A good way to start is to visit the greenhouses of nurserymen in the fall when their mums are growing for the commercial trade and select the types and colors that are most pleasing. There are many shades of yellow, pink, lavender, bronze, and even white, and some like the shaggy type while others prefer the tight, incurved ball shape. About the only thing the outdoor growers agree on is the size —the bigger the better, at least in the beginning. Later on the finer points of shape, texture, refinement, and purity of color come into their own, and without too much sacrifice of size.

Naturally the earlier-maturing types must be selected for outdoor culture, since under no circumstances, however favorable from the standpoint of weather, can the season be stretched out beyond the middle of November.

Most nurserymen are willing to sell rooted cuttings from their mums in the spring, but unfortunately in most cases they do not start rooting these cuttings until late June so that they are not available until about July 1. This is ample time for indoor forcing but a little late for outdoor growing. However, with careful handling splendid blooms can be had, even though the stems may be a trifle shorter than desired. After the first season, of course, the grower can make his own cuttings as early as he wants them.

In preparing the bed for these mums it is well to see that the soil is conditioned a bit because the mums are gross feeders. They require a well-drained, porous soil, and, if possible, natural protection from high winds. Well-rotted cow manure, broken decayed sod, and finely ground bone meal are especially valuable in preparing the bed, and should be dug in to a depth not exceeding 8 or 10 inches, as the roots stay pretty close to the surface at all times.

In staking out a bed, consideration must be given to the later erection of a frost tent, which, as its name denotes, is a protection against frost and also heavy rain and high winds. A light frost does no harm to closed buds or foliage but does injure open blooms. The tent also protects the open blooms from rain, as, if stretched fairly tight, it acts like an umbrella, and permits only a fine mist to spray through. A few cheap wooden posts with cross-pieces and a muslin cover that will come to maybe two feet from the ground on all four sides are all that is required. This tent is put down every night as the time for frost approaches and raised in the morning if the sun is up nicely. It is put down during the day if it is raining or very windy. Leaving the tent over the plants does not retard development of the buds but, on the contrary, tends to hasten it. If the bed is located adjacent to the house, a garage, or other building, then, of course, protection is needed on only three sides.

Having located and prepared the bed, the cuttings are planted in rows, being careful to have such rows perfectly straight in order to facilitate supporting the plants as they grow. It will be found most convenient and desirable from all angles to place the plants about 12 inches apart and the rows about 10 inches apart. Closer planting makes cultivating more difficult and requires more frequent fertilizing. If the bed is long, it is best to leave a space say every 4 feet or so as a path from which to disbud or otherwise take care of the plants. This, at first, may seem to be sacrificing space which could be used for plants, but the risk of breaking off buds is very great when one has to reach over the tops very far. The tips of a good healthy plant are very brittle, and often the mere brushing of an elbow or hand will snap it off.

The purchased cuttings can, of course, be very simply kept to a single stem. When they get to be about 12 inches tall, the most common practice is to pinch off the tip. Almost immediately a new shoot or shoots will start from the side, and the best is selected to continue and the others rubbed off. From now on the job is to keep the plants growing steadily. The soil should never be permitted to dry out. Along about mid-August a mulch of well-rotted horse or cow manure, an inch or so deep, can be spread over the bed. Staking the plants will be necessary, and the method used depends on how many plants there are. If there are not too many, bamboo canes such as are used for staking tall plants can be used, but if there are many plants ingenious methods of running rope lengthwise and tying the plants to it have been used. The interested gardener usually has his own methods and all of them are good. Provision must be made, however, to raise the support as the plants grow and the head opens and becomes heavy.

Most varieties of the exhibition-sized mums throw their best blooms from the crown bud, which is a single bud at the tip of the stalk and generally makes its appearance late in August or early in September. Other shoots will appear from the sides, with clusters of buds at the tip, and these must be rubbed off as soon as they become large enough to do so without injury to the main stem. It is prudent, however, to leave a shoot somewhere near the top in case the crown bud is accidentally knocked off. This reserve shoot can be rubbed off when it gets long and another permitted to start up. Shoots will also start from the roots, and these should be cut off, as they sap the plant and diminish the size of the blooms. When the bloom has reached a good size, however, these shoots, which furnish next year's plants, can be permitted to grow.

When the buds get to be the size of a dime, a feeding of liquid manure, composed of diluted dry cow or horse manure having the appearance of weak coffee, can be given once or twice a week. Most gardeners use a small receptacle and apply the liquid direct to the base of the individual plants. The liquid should be prepared in a fairly large quantity and permitted to stand a week or so before using. As soon as the buds show color, this feeding is stopped.

By now an examination will show that the base of the stem is definitely brown and woody and the lower several tiers of leaves are drying up. The upper leaves should be dark green, firm in texture, and healthy looking, and the stem thick enough to support the heavy flower. Every gardener has his own list of "do's" and "don'ts," and while most of them have merit, the ordinary use of common sense and the value of experience contribute much to success.

Some very early varieties can be brought to maturity without the protection of the frost tent, but even with those there is still the danger of destruction by a heavy and sudden downpour or a gale of high proportions. In general, however, Labor Day is a good day for erecting the frost tent and starting its use.

From here on the job consists mainly of keeping

the little side shoots off and the soil a little bit on the dry side. If the soil is permitted to remain wet the blooms will "shatter" easily and not last long when cut. Usually the normal rainfall and the occasional applications of liquid manure are sufficient. If it becomes necessary to supply water, it should be done *at the roots,* and the soaking should be a good one.

Since the roots will be taken up the following year and broken up and replanted, if they have not been labeled as to name or color, now is the time to do it, so identity will not be lost.

As soon as all blooms have been cut, the main stem is shortened to about 3 or 4 inches and labeled. When the ground has frozen fairly solid, the plants can be covered with straw or, preferably, salt hay. In this latitude (northern New Jersey) the mulch should be several inches deep. The use of leaves is not to be recommended, as they tend to mat and smother the plants.

Along about May 1 the covering may be removed and the roots permitted to send up shoots. Memorial Day is a good time to dig up the roots and prepare the bed for another season. The new shoots are carefully detached and planted again as single stems. This second year will have two distinct advantages. First, you can get the plants started earlier and before the very hot, dry spell comes on; second, it is commonly felt that these sprouts from the roots are better adapted to outdoor culture than rooted cuttings. At any rate they seem to react to transplanting more favorably than do the cuttings.

Between the two seasons the gardener probably will have seen some varieties he would like to add to his bed, and these can be purchased when available. In the windows of florists' shops one will often see a fine collection of blooms, and usually the proprietor of the store can, and will be glad to, give the inquirer the names of varieties.

Don't set out these big fellows unless you want the neighbors, and a lot of people who are not neighbors, trooping into your garden to see and admire them. It takes all summer to get to the place where you can stand back and enjoy your work, and the season even then is a short one; but the final reward is worth the effort.

Many flower lovers who come to admire the outdoor exhibitions of large chrysanthemums in the gardens of those who have had a successful season and have brought them to full bloom and beauty before the freezing weather sets in are enthusiastic about the idea of duplicating the effort in their own back yards until they give some real thought to the problems involved, and then as a general proposition they decide that the smaller hardy chrysanthemum, which thrives in just ordinarily good soil, average rainfall, and a not too exacting amount of attention, will fill the bill very nicely.

Many feel that their nice back-yard gardens would not be enhanced by anything but a well-

Rose Glow is an odd raspberry-rose of vigorous growth, and profuse bloom in September. Two feet.

LAVENDER LADY, of a distinct real lavender hue, is deservedly one of the most popular of all hardy mums. Unexcelled for cutting, and for mixed bouquets.

constructed and permanent frame for the frost tent, and rightly so. And they want a frost tent that, when it is lowered and fastened, will be neat and no more unattractive than possible. Also the thought of the effort and vigilance required to protect the blooms each night from frost, and perhaps dropping the curtain during the day if a heavy rainfall or even snowfall is imminent, doesn't do much to encourage going ahead with large blooms. If the wife, who is around the house all day, is the enthusiast, the job is made somewhat more simple; but if it is the husband who is the ardent one, he's got to get full co-operation from those at home when he is away at his office or out of town. That is, unless he doesn't mind groping around in the dark, fastening the tent securely against the elements.

Nor should those who close up their homes for the summer or those who go away for a month or more try to raise these large mums unless they can induce someone to come around at least once a week to see that they are watered, staked up, sprayed against aphis, and kept trimmed to one stalk and one bud.

It is mainly for these reasons that the gardener who specializes in these large blooms soon comes to the conclusion that while it is no trouble to find folks who will cart home an armful of flowers in the fall, there aren't many waiting for his excess plants in the spring. Growing these large blooms outdoors is only for people who want to do something different, and who are able and willing to do a little extra work for results that are gratifying and often profit able.

GARDEN CHRYSANTHEMUMS UNDER GREENHOUSE CULTURE

Perhaps you wonder why your favorite garden chrysanthemums are not seen more in the florist shop. Commercial kinds, however, are not selected with beauty as the first requisite. Production must be considered; substance is equally important, since flowers are usually handled by the grower, wholesaler, and the retail florist, in turn, before they reach the purchaser. Their selection, therefore, is limited to the kinds that can stand repeated handling.

For local use, these considerations are of less importance, which paves the way for a daintier, less commonplace choice. Many of the garden types fit in here nicely, particularly the Korean Hybrids, with their unusual pastel coloring.

A number of large commercial growers are now featuring the Korean Hybrid type, flowering them successfully in protected cold frames and following this crop with another in the greenhouse. While it may appear logical to assume that garden varieties grown in the greenhouse will flower earlier than they would outside, the fact is that they are invariably ten to fourteen days later. Just why this is so has not been satisfactorily determined. Perhaps it is because in the greenhouse they do not get the full benefit of the cool nights during autumn; hence a somewhat later bud formation or ripening takes place.

COLD-FRAME CULTURE

The cold frame, if not otherwise needed, may be used to advantage to assure good blooming, particularly in sections where severe early frosts are apt to occur. All that is required is a light framework upon which to rest the sash that is used to protect the plants from excessive rain and later from frost. Tobacco cloth or heavy cheesecloth, tacked on the sides and ends, will furnish more protection from cold than one might expect. Chrysanthemums grown in cold frames will flower about the same date as they would if grown in the open garden. The advantages of the cold-frame treatment are a sure crop, flowers of better quality, and a degree of immunity to some of the insect pests.

In the greenhouse the same advantages are obtained, but here later-flowering kinds may be used to prolong the season.

It will be obvious that if one particularly wants cut chrysanthemums, a long season of them can be managed. Whether grown in a frame, under shade treatment, or in the greenhouse, the objective will be to cut as many good flowers as possible from the available space. Planting out in 6 to 8 inches of good rich soil and spacing the plants about 9 inches apart are the usual practice. Since we are dealing with garden varieties, large natural sprays will be the aim. The plants should not be pinched as often as recommended for garden culture. Five to seven shoots or main stems will be ample. Surplus growths should be removed early in the season when 2 or 3 inches long. Attention to staking will be in order by midsummer. The heavy branches full of flower buds may need extra support later.

With quantity again in mind, there will be no advantage in disbudding for size of individual blooms, as is practiced with the larger types and occasionally with Pompon varieties. By removing most of the buds, leaving only one or two to a spray, the size of the Pompons is often more than doubled —an illogical practice, it must be admitted, since the whole charm of the Pompon lies in its diminutive perfection. These garden varieties, more lusty and branching than the average greenhouse sorts, because of their dense growth, require careful attention not only in watering but in spraying. Neglect of any sort is almost sure to induce foliage disease.

The practice of frequently spraying with water —at one time sound—is not now recommended. It brings about conditions under which the nematode thrives and is, of course, conducive to mildew and other fungous diseases. Spray as you would for other garden pests, but do not wait until they appear. Prevention is by far the easier course. Make it a point, then, to spray every ten days, using your judgment as to whether an insecticide or a fungicide spray is needed. If a contact spray, such as nicotine and soap, is applied regularly and good culture is maintained until the buds show some color, this will forestall disease and assure flowers of the finest quality. The old gardener's adage, "Spray when it ain't needed," still holds good.

GARDEN CHRYSANTHEMUMS IN POTS

As mentioned elsewhere, it is entirely practical to grow plants in the vegetable or service garden during the summer, keeping them dwarf and stocky by pinching; dig with ball of soil and pot in early September, or just about the time buds are forming. Water well, of course. This method is the best where a few plants are needed, because it disposes of the continual attention to watering necessary during summer. Where large quantities are involved, it would be well to start with cuttings or small plants from 2¼-inch pots in early spring, shifting these to larger sizes as they attain growth.

The following varieties will be found excellent for pot culture:

Single Koreans: Apollo, Autumn Lights, Ceres, Daphne, Orion, Louise Schling, and Nancy Copeland.

Double Koreans: Burgundy, Caliph, Indian Summer, King Midas, Magnolia, Mrs. Pierre S. DuPont, III, and Red Velvet are also fine for this purpose.

111

HARDY CHRYSANTHEMUMS

In addition to these mentioned here, any of the good free-flowering garden kinds can be used. The Pompon varieties Early Bronze, Judith Anderson, Jewell, and Pomponette, being stocky in habit, are particularly well adapted for pot culture.

CHAPTER V

DISEASES AND INSECTS

U NDER garden cultivation chrysanthemums are almost immune to the fungous diseases which sometimes seriously affect them under glass. Crowded plantings, poor soil condition, or lack of sufficient water may cause trouble, however. A few of the more important ailments are mentioned here.

DISEASES

Mildew

The familiar powdery white mold, which appears on roses, phlox, and many other plants in early summer, sometimes spreads to the chrysanthemums. It is not difficult to dispose of. Sulphur dust is effective if applied promptly. Tri-ogen is also good, and often just a soap spray, applied lukewarm, will check a mild attack. When all other sprays fail, try liver of sulphur (potassium sulphide), 1 ounce to 3 gallons of water. Soap may be added if desired. This we have found the most effective spray for mildew on any plant. It will discolor painted woodwork, so care must be exercised when using it near garden furniture or garden labels. Recently a correspondent reported excellent results from using liver of sulphur double strength. To quote, "Plants in July getting leggier and leggier, foliage spotted and badly blighted. Badly affected leaves were removed before spraying." Heroic treatment this, but the results evidently were satisfactory, for to quote again, "The foliage seemed to improve immediately and the lower leaves are green to this day—October 10. The plants in flower and breathtakingly beautiful."

Rust

This is indicated by the appearance of blisters, on both the upper and lower leaf surface, from which dark-brown spores emanate and quickly spread to adjoining plants. Affected leaves will be noted by the ugly brown patches. These leaves should be removed and a sulphur dust applied; or the liver of sulphur spray mentioned for mildew may be used. Like leaf spot and other fungous diseases rust is largely caused by crowding among other plants, poorly drained soil, or stuffy air conditions.

Leaf Spot

Small brownish to black spots are noted first. The leaves soon turn yellow and drop off. The disease appears first on the lower leaves and rapidly works

RESULT OF NEMATODE or eel-worm infestation. Insert shows infested leaf with pronounced blotch, a sure indication of the affliction.

Louise Schling, strong-growing and free-flowering semi-double, is a favorite for mass planting for landscape effects.

up through the plant. Plants may be affected to the extent that they soon become partially denuded of foliage. Here again unhealthy plants, congested growing conditions, or too much moisture on the foliage may be responsible. Remove all affected foliage and spray with Bordeaux mixture.

Fermate, a new organic sulphur fungicide used with excellent success as a control for cedar rust on apples, anthracnose on tomatoes and beans, has proven highly satisfactory in controlling leaf spot on mums, using it at the rate of 1 pound per 100 gallons (with DuPont Spreader Sticker), 1 to 3000. As a control for black spot and mildew on roses, with the addition of 20 per cent sulphur, results were again excellent, which indicates that fermate used throughout the season may control to a large extent all foliage diseases affecting the chrysanthemum.

There are other fungous diseases of similar nature, but none seriously affects the chrysanthemum. Tri-ogen is a good preventive, and, as suggested elsewhere, it is good practice when spraying roses in June, or later, to give the chrysanthemums an application by way of forestalling trouble. Bordeaux mixture is a splendid control for nearly all fungous diseases. Apparently, though, its persistent use stunts the growth. I have noticed this effect also after application of too strong a solution.

Leaf Drop

Occasionally plants, particularly after an exuberance of rapid growth, will show a tendency to drop their lower leaves. This condition may develop suddenly. This has been reported as a bacteriological disease, but my impression is that the bacteriological infection is not the cause but an after-effect.

It is doubtless the result of some extreme condition—too much moisture or, more often, lack of sufficient moisture *under the plant*—soil too loose, or too much fertilizer, either of which might affect the tender feeding rootlets and cause a sudden stoppage in the flow of moisture and food elements. Since this condition appears with humid dry weather in the garden, but never on chrysanthemums growing under glass or in frames where water is available, the premise seems justified.

We are again brought back to "good culture" as the answer. Avoid overcrowding; when water is needed, *water thoroughly,* and keep the plants properly divided and young.

If a bacterial infection is indicated, spray with Bordeaux mixture.

INSECT PESTS

Fortunately the garden chrysanthemum is comparatively free from insect depredations, to a large extent escaping the pests that are troublesome under greenhouse conditions. Doubtless this is because they do not have to contend with the stuffy atmospheric condition, which is almost sure to prevail in some corner of the greenhouse, because of poor ventilation. It is in these favorable spots that insects establish themselves and then increase rapidly. Here fungous and foliage diseases also first appear.

For this reason the gardener will avoid wall corners and pockets out of doors where air circulation is poor. If, as sometimes happens, chrysanthemums must be planted under these conditions, both insects and diseases are to be carefully watched for. With prevention in mind, spray often, alternating contact insecticide with fungicide sprays.

NEMATODES

Within recent years the nematode has become troublesome in many gardens. Identified by the Department of Nematology at Washington as the chrysanthemum strain of the bud and leaf nematode (*Asphelenchoides fragariae*), it is in everyday language a minute form of eelworm living within the leaf tissue, therefore invisible, and immune to surface or contact spray.

Badly infected plants may be almost totally defoliated by October, little remaining except half-opened, deformed blossoms. Since a similar defoliation may be the result of leaf spot, crowding among other plants, or generally poor culture, a study of nematode symptoms is worth while, for it is a serious pest.

The nematode hibernates over winter in the plant stolons or runners, usually around the buds or in dry leaves and stems of the previous season, from which it travels to the young growths in early summer. Of particular interest is the fact that it lacks the usual means of locomotion, but *swims* from leaf to leaf. This it can do, of course, only when moisture is present. Eggs are deposited within the leaf structure, the larvae developing in about ten days and feeding within the leaf where a spray will not reach them.

First symptoms appear usually in June, following a moist, warm period. Brown patches appear on the lower leaves, either on one or both sides of the leaf, always working toward the tip *in definite bands* rather than blotches, never crossing the leaf ribs. (This distinguishes nematodes from leaf spot, a fungous disease.) Soon several of the lower leaves will turn brown. Following each moist period more injury will appear, likely very serious in the event of a wet summer.

Prevention

Remove affected foliage promptly. Send some leaves to your agricultural experiment station and ask for a nematode examination. Avoid syringing or any application of water to the foliage, particularly when watering. Remove and burn before winter all stems, fallen leaves, and rubbish in which the nematode might overwinter.

Remedy

Unfortunately no one remedy is available for the nematode. Spraying with Bordeaux and nicotine, the latter double strength, will check movement on the leaf surface and prevent rapid spread of the pest. Objection to this treatment—it disfigures the plant, and may check its growth.

Montague Free, horticulturist of the Brooklyn Botanic Garden, reports "excellent success by using tobacco dust, applying a half-inch mulch in early spring, and keeping all infested areas completely covered throughout the season."

The treatment developed by Dr. B. O. Dodge, of the New York Botanical Garden, involves the removal of all plants, working over and pulverizing the soil to a depth of 3 inches, then drenching thoroughly with a 1 to 100 solution of 40 per cent formaldehyde, using the dilution at the rate of ½ gallon to each square foot. To ensure penetration, the treated areas should be covered promptly with heavy paper, canvas, old blankets, or a 1-inch covering of uninfested soil. Peat moss undoubtedly would be effective as a covering, and certainly beneficial to the soil. Two or three days after treatment the soil should be dug over and allowed to aerate two or three more days before planting. It is recommended that all infested plants be destroyed and replaced with healthy stock.

This treatment, aside from the labor involved, is not expensive. It disposed of the nematode infestation at the New York Botanical Garden when it was so bad that the chrysanthemums were more or less crippled for several successive seasons. Doubtless other benefits resulting from the treatment would more than justify its use.

Experiments now under way by Dr. W. E. Blauvelt and Professor A. W. Dimock of Cornell University promise perhaps a more simple solution. Sodium selenate, in very dilute amounts, is watered thoroughly into the soil. Absorbed by the plant, apparently it destroys the nematode. It also immunizes the plant from further infestation of this as well as several other insect pests.

Another promising new nematode killer, known as Emulsified D.D., developed and announced by the Agricultural Research Administration of the Department of Agriculture, has evidently worked out successfully in combating the sugar beet nematode. Let us hope it will prove equally valuable for chrysanthemums and other garden plants subject to nematode injury.

If this treatment works out satisfactorily, it would be possible for the amateur to at least treat a plant or two of each variety, propagating additional stock from the treated plants. In the meantime, soil in definite areas of the garden could be sterilized for the reception of these nematode-free plants if they cannot be removed to areas in which chrysanthemums were not previously grown.

Where the presence of nematodes is suspected, I would suggest using at least the tobacco-dust mulch, being sure that it is kept in close contact with all growths, thus making it difficult for the nematode to work its way up the stems during moist weather. Tobacco applied in this way is an excellent fertilizer and soil rectifier and should be more generally used, regardless of nematodes.

Commercial growers can eliminate nematode infestation by sterilizing dormant plants with a hot-water treatment similar to that used for narcissus bulbs. Equipment is now manufactured for this purpose, but for small-scale operations a metal tank or metal mortar box will work satisfactorily if a tight matched board covering is made and kept well weighted during the treatment period. Sufficient water should be used to ensure complete coverage of every part of the plant. To be effective a temperature of 115 degrees must be maintained for fifteen minutes. An eighteen-minute submersion is, I think, surer and reasonably safe. Steam, conducted by hose, is the best way to bring the water to the right temperature, and since the addition of a quantity of plants will cause a drop of a degree or two, it is better to start at 117 degrees. Cover promptly and tightly, and maintain the 115-degree temperature through the required period, with a leeway of not more than 1½ degrees allowable. It is important to use tested thermometers. *Check the water every five minutes,* and add steam if necessary.

Notwithstanding the fact that some of the plants may be injured by the treatment, it is the surest way devised so far to eliminate this pest. Great care should be taken that these treated plants or stock propagated therefrom will not be recontaminated. Propagating sand, soils, and all materials employed thereafter—even the flowerpots, if previously used —should be sterilized. Equally important, these treated plants should be planted in soil not previously used for chrysanthemums.

Selective propagation might be considered too. Since the nematode is inactive when the temperature is below 70 degrees, it is not likely to spread through the plant until early summer. Tip cuttings from the soft, early spring growths are, therefore, usually clean. Cuttings from these planted in sterilized sand and container should, if possible, be again transplanted to sterilized soil. However, under normal garden conditions they would unquestionably make better plants than divisions from affected stock.

Certain sanitary practices should be observed to discourage nematode spread. Over winter the nematode attaches itself to stolons, roots, or to the leaves near the soil surface, but seldom penetrates the soil for more than 1 or 2 inches. It has remarkable vitality. Bouen, a Dutch investigator, reports that

CHARMING IN THEIR simplicity are the daisy-like glistening white blooms of Silver Moon, which has fragrance as an added attraction.

Autumn Lights has the distinction of being the hardiest
of all bronze-colored outdoor chrysanthemums.

he kept infested dry leaves in a desk drawer for five years; then he revived a number of specimens. Where infestations exist, every sanitary precaution should be taken. In late fall stems, leaves, and any stem particles should be cleared from the garden and immediately burned.

Aphis (*Plant Lice, Green Fly*)

During late spring and again when the cool nights of autumn approach, aphis are usually seen on the more tender tips of the growths, as well as the underside of the leaves of the chrysanthemums. Sometimes completely covering the stems, they are easily recognized. They may be green, reddish tinted, or black. They breed rapidly, sucking the plant juices. As the lice are voracious feeders, the plants soon become weakened, and malformed foliage appears. Fortunately aphis are readily disposed of with any good contact spray. Black Leaf 40, used 50 per cent stronger than recommended on the container; or liquid Nico-fume, diluted at the rate of 1 ounce to 4 gallons of water, will promptly destroy them. Soap should be added, about 2 heaping tablespoonfuls per gallon, using lukewarm water. Apply late or early in the day, drenching the foliage above and beneath.

Chrysanthemum Midge

The midge, a troublesome greenhouse pest, is now making considerable headway in the garden in some sections. Its presence is indicated by the appearance of lumpy galls or swellings on the upper leaf surface. Orange-colored eggs are deposited on the leaf by the female fly; the larvae, which hatch in from one to two weeks, immediately penetrate the leaf tissue, where their development causes the lumpy condition mentioned. After about twenty-eight days the fly emerges, usually after nightfall, and promptly proceeds to deposit eggs. A light infestation of the garden does no great harm other than to disfigure the foliage. A contact spray will destroy the eggs, but to eradicate the midge completely, persistent spraying is needed.

In the greenhouse, where midge is a serious pest, it can be best eliminated with a course of treatment, starting in winter with the stock plants. These are severely cut back after flowering, all infected leaves removed, and then segregated where they can be sprayed every third day, for three weeks; then once a week. (Use Loro according to manufacturer's directions.) New growth is gone over carefully and all infested foliage removed and burned. Once the midge is eliminated, the grower will want to prevent reinfestation from new plants secured from other sources. He makes sure they are midge free. Nicotine plus soap, or any good standard rotenone spray, if used consistently, will prove effective as a control.

Thrips

Too minute to be seen with the naked eye, the presence of the thrips is manifested by the appearance of white spots on the foliage at the growth tips. The leaf soon becomes discolored and then dies. In feeding, the insect sucks the plant juices, leaving a noticeable gummy liquid residue on the leaf surface. The thrip requires a dry condition of the atmosphere for its spread. It is apt to be found on starved plants or in stuffy, congested corners where air circulation is poor.

Pyrethrum sprays are apparently effective; so also is Nico-fume, with the addition of soap. One heaping teaspoonful Paris green, 1 cup molasses (or 1 tablespoonful brown sugar) to 1½ gallons lukewarm water is an effective remedy. Either of these solutions should be repeated at least once a week until all traces of new injury disappear. Spray should be applied forcibly down into the leaf tips as well as from beneath.

Red Spider

Like the thrips, this pest is almost invisible to the naked eye. It thrives under the same conditions. Spider, however, works on the underside of the leaf, and as it multiplies with amazing rapidity, an infestation soon becomes serious. A gray webbing indicates its presence. Soon the leaf becomes yellow and blotched. A lens or good reading glass will make identification possible; with it the plump reddish insects are readily seen. A strong nicotine spray plus soap, applied every three days, will be found effective control.

Tarnished Plant Bug

The presence of this pest is easily noted by wilting and malformation of the top growths. Look for a small yellow-and-brown bug about ¼ inch in length. The adult is active and, for that reason, difficult to hit with a spray. It is equipped with a long proboscis which penetrates the stem, damaging the tender tissues to the extent that affected shoots seldom produce good flowers. In the younger stages the insects can be seen on the underside of the leaf where they can be hit with a spray. Fortunately this insect is most active during hot summer weather and seldom does much injury to chrysanthemums in the garden, except the very early kinds.

Pyrethrum sprays are fairly effective. The nicotine and soap acts as a repellent but is effective for only a few days and, therefore, should be applied frequently if the insects are plentiful. Hand-picking in the morning is the surest remedy.

Caterpillars

Many types of these, starting with the tent caterpillar in late spring and followed by others that appear sporadically through summer, may cause temporary injury. Healthy plants, however, soon outgrow this. A poison spray may be required if the damage is considerable. Arsenate of lead, used as the maker directs, is the surest remedy, but it will discolor the plant for several weeks. If but a few plants are concerned, hand-picking is advised. Plants should be well looked over at night, however, with a good flashlight, as many caterpillars are night feeders.

Snails and Slugs

Sometimes these garden pests are troublesome on young chrysanthemum plants in early spring and again on stock plants being carried over in cold frames or in the greenhouse. They can be caught and destroyed readily on a dark, cloudy night. Arsenate of lead is an effective remedy. As it is used early in the season, the discoloring is not objectionable.

Cutworms

The worst of all night-feeding pests, the cutworm often destroys young chrysanthemums as well as many other plants. Poison baits are not effective in the garden, because the cutworms prefer the young growing plants to the bait. Poison sprays are reasonably effective, but much damage is done before they are disposed of. Being night feeders, they can best be caught sometime after dark. After feeding, they conceal themselves in the soil, and seldom travel far from the plant on which they feed. Where feeding is indicated the previous night, turn up the soil to a depth of an inch or so within a radius of about a foot of the plant. They can then be found, curled up so tightly that often they are not immediately detected. Inasmuch as a single cutworm will destroy a number of young plants overnight, it is worth while hunting for them.

INSECTICIDES AND FUNGICIDES

It is well to realize that several types of insecticides are necessary to cover the requirements of the garden. Poison sprays are used for insects that chew or eat the foliage. These include cutworms, caterpillars of various kinds, grasshoppers, leaf rollers, and some sorts of beetles. A number of prepared poison sprays, which can be applied with little trouble, are available.

Nicotine

Of the various contact sprays there are none so effective as nicotine sulphate in some form. Black Leaf 40, which can readily be bought from any local seedsman, florist, or hardware merchant, is thoroughly efficient.

Soap

The addition of soap as a spreader is important, particularly where nicotine is used as a spray. It not only produces a finer, more misty spray but it causes the material to adhere better to smooth-bodied insects and foliage; thus it adds to the effectiveness of any contact insecticide with which it may be used. It also helps to prevent possible scalding or burning of the foliage. Any of the good household soaps may be used. The flake brands dissolve rapidly in warm water and should be applied in a semi-warm or tepid state.

Whale-oil Soap

Its overpowering odor, plus the fact that it is slow to dissolve, discourages the more general use of this old-time specific. When other insecticides fail, however—as they often do, in such cases as an infestation of those tough midsummer aphis which appear on Van Houtte spiraea or the European cranberry bush; or if red spider gets the upper hand —then the substitution of whale oil for the usual soap used in the contact spray will kill. After an application of whale-oil soap it will be noticed that the foliage has taken on a healthy, luxuriant appearance, indicating that it may carry some needed food element which is absorbed by the foliage. Anyway, the general appearance of well-being which the plant acquires more than compensates for the truly "gosh-awful" odor.

Liver of Sulphur (Potassium Sulphide)

This is the most effective remedy, to my knowledge, for mildew on chrysanthemums or any other plant. The principal objection to its use is that it leaves a yellow stain on painted woodwork and renders garden labels unreadable, unless they are covered while spraying is in progress. It comes in rock form and loses its strength rapidly unless kept in a cool place and in a tight container. It is best to get it weighed out in the quantity desired when it is wanted for use. Wholesale drugstores can supply it fresh. I find it most convenient to let it dissolve, which it does slowly, in a quart jar of water. One ounce is used to 3 gallons of water, in which a cupful of soap chips has been dissolved. Thoroughly drench the foliage above and underneath. Two applications within three or four days will check the most stubborn case of mildew. It may be used somewhat stronger for the second application.

Arsenical Compounds

Arsenate of lead, the best known of these, is effective and safe. Its one objection is that it discolors foliage for a few weeks. Its continued use may stunt the growth. The use of soap with arsenical compounds is not advised.

Hellebore

This is an old stand-by as a dust. It can be applied in liquid form to excellent advantage by dissolving 1 ounce in 1 quart of hot water. Dilute with 3 quarts of water and apply freely.

ABOVE (*left*), freshly made cuttings with lower leaves removed ready for inserting in rooting medium. *Right,* rooted, ready for potting or transplanting. Below, cuttings inserted in sand in a bulb pan. This is a simple and sure method of propagating. Water in the saucer keeps the sand constantly and evenly moist.

LEFT, a 3-inch pot plant, ideal planting size, and ready for first pinching back. RIGHT, perfect plant, in August, from 3-inch pot plant set out in June. Given first pinch back when 6 inches high, last when 12 to 15 inches high, in mid-July. Branching growth,

DISEASES AND INSECTS

Paris Green

Another old stand-by that is one of the most effective poison sprays. But it requires care in handling or plant injury may occur. It is dangerous material to have on hand, and with the number of prepared poison sprays now readily available, Paris green hardly need be used.

Contact sprays are used for sucking insects— aphis, plant lice of various types, red spider, and a number of mites too small to see with the naked eye. The contact spray kills by completely enveloping and smothering the insect, or by its caustic effect on the tissues; therefore, the spraying must be well done to be effective. Here is where a good pump is necessary.

Non-poison Sprays

There are several good "non-poison" sprays, that is, not poisonous to humans or animals. Of these pyrethrum and rotenone form the base. Being non-poisonous, they can be kept safely anywhere, and for uses where they prove effective, they should be employed in preference to those which are dangerous.

Sulphur Dust

"Dusting" sulphur, as it is now prepared especially for this purpose, is much more effective than were the older forms. An excellent preventive for mildew, blights, and other fungous diseases, it is also a convenient treatment. For garden use get a "dusting" brand from your seed dealer or florist, rather than the drugstore kind, which is not sufficiently fine to do a good job.

CHAPTER VI

PROPAGATION

PROPAGATION BY MEANS OF CUTTINGS

Chrysanthemums are so easily and rapidly increased by division of the old plant—the most natural way—that it is generally unnecessary to resort to cuttings or slips. Cuttings are not difficult to root, however. They may be taken from the growing plants in the garden any time from spring until mid-June.

A pet plant which the gardener is anxious to increase may be started into growth in the house as early as mid-January. In this case, the plant is potted in late fall, using a 6- or 7-inch flowerpot or an azalea pot, and kept in a protected cold frame until January, when it is brought into a warm temperature. It is impossible, however, to hold plants over successfully in an ordinary cellar, because whenever the temperature approaches the 40-degree mark growth will start. It will be a weedy, watery growth unless the plants are in a good light and getting normal air circulation. Therefore, it is better to keep the plants in a cool, well-lighted room than under cellar conditions. A night temperature of about 55 degrees is ideal, but the plants will stand a somewhat higher temperature fairly well.

In years past the details of making the cutting—just where and how the cut should be made, et cetera—were unduly stressed. This is relatively unimportant; success depends more upon aftercare. Cuttings are best taken when the growth is 4 to 5 inches high, using the soft tip growth. They are usually made 3 or 4 inches long. The cut can be made anywhere at, or between, the nodes, where the stem is soft. All leaves are removed from the lower 2 inches or so of the cutting, in order that it may be planted without the remaining foliage touching the sand.

Under greenhouse conditions a night temperature of 50 or 55 degrees, with the sand temperature 5 or 6 degrees higher, is ideal for rooting. In the home, however, this is difficult to approximate, but the important thing is to avoid drafty conditions, such as an open window or ventilator may cause. Avoid also such extreme heat as occurs close to a radiator. The chrysanthemum is, after all, a cool-blooded plant, and it is better to err on the cool side. Use the right rooting material. That is important. Either pure clean sand, or a half-and-half mixture of sand and imported peat moss, will do. Soil or enrichment of any sort should be avoided. All that is required is a clean, bacteria-free medium that will hold the moisture necessary to keep the cuttings alive until roots are made.

A bulb pan or shallow flowerpot makes an excellent container for the rooting medium, but I have seen cuttings rooted successfully in saucers and baking utensils. The sand or sand-and-peat mixture should be pressed firmly into the container, drainage first being supplied by using a layer of broken pots, cinders, or crushed stone. The cuttings can be dibbled in tightly about 2 inches apart, using a lead pencil as a convenient tool. Then water thoroughly. A 6-inch pan will hold fifteen to twenty cuttings.

Too much sprinkling or syringing can easily start damping off and fungous infection. This can be avoided by placing the pan in a deep saucer or a soup plate. Use this container as a reservoir and keep it always partially filled with water until new growth starts; then withhold the water gradually. Watch always for the first sign of foliage wilt, covering then with damp newspaper until the leaves freshen up. Above all, avoid drafty spots and heat extremes. In three or four weeks new roots should have started. Then the cuttings can be transferred to pots or boxes with a good growing soil. If weather permits, they may be planted directly in a cold frame, 4 inches apart, and kept shaded and fairly close until growth commences. Then they should be gradually ventilated and thus hardened off, as early as possible, in preparation for later transplanting to the open.

HARDY CHRYSANTHEMUMS

The recent development of idolebutyric acid and other root-growth preparations offers a means of speeding up the rooting process by several days and assures a more successful strike. Sold under various trade names, these preparations are proving valuable particularly on certain groups that are slow and difficult to propagate. Under even average conditions chrysanthemum cuttings root so readily that chemical aids are not usually required.

GROWING CHRYSANTHEMUMS FROM SEED

To many there is a certain fascination in growing chrysanthemums from seed, a tantalizing element of chance. So if you are not concerned as to definite shades or colors, but simply want a lot of flowers in all colors, then by all means try the Korean Hybrids from seed. I particularly specify these, because they are generally hardier and will produce a far greater range of color than any other strain that I know. Get your seed, however, from a good source, collected from selected or pedigreed parents, rather than just "run of the field." A choice strain, in addition to producing the best possible range of colors and types of plant, will be likely to offer some very superior kinds. A good strain may cost three or four times as much as a poor one but is well worth the difference.

Seed sown by early March will make good flowering plants the same season, even in New England. Drainage such as is used for cuttings should be provided, and the compost should be light—one third sand, one third peat moss, and one third good mellow loam. For small amounts the bulb pan is again the best container, although a deep cigar box will do. After supplying drainage, fill the container to within ½ inch of the top, pressing the mixture firmly with the hand. Level it, then screen through a flour sieve a light top covering. Sow the seed, and press gently to firm it in. For this purpose the flat bottom of a baking-powder or other can will serve. Chrysanthemum seeds, being fine, require very little top covering; 1/16 inch is sufficient.

Overhead watering, even with a fine sprinkler, is apt to wash and expose the seeds. It is better to set the container in a basin of water until the upper surface is moist. This applies also after germination occurs. Germination requires two to four weeks. In some two to three weeks more, the character leaf having developed, the seedlings can be transplanted to pans, flats, or boxes, in which they are spaced 2 inches apart. A second transplanting is made in late April or early May to the cold frame or, farther South, to a sheltered spot directly in the garden. Immediately after transplanting, cover with moist newspaper to prevent undue wilting. In a few days new feeding roots will have been made, and the plants can be hardened off and given all the sunshine possible.

CHAPTER VII

CHRYSANTHEMUM BREEDING

ABOUT PLANT BREEDING

Plant breeding, if carried out on scientific lines, is a decidedly involved process. A thorough understanding of the causes of variation and the linkage of inherited characters is essential.

The commercial breeder, however, is usually more concerned with getting results than with any exact pattern of scientific methods. Experimental work of this kind soon runs into considerable expense. Logically, the plant breeder's work, unless subsidized in some way, must pay for itself. At this moment I cannot think of any commercial breeder operating under such happy circumstance as a subsidy. The scientific breeder—and I have the greatest respect and admiration for him—is concerned with the mysterious workings of the genes and the chromosomes; he delves into the causes of variation. His mission in life is not to produce some outstanding hybrid that will startle the horticultural world and bring him fame and adulation for

Mercury, the first Hybrid Korean chrysanthemum to be introduced, and forerunner of present-day varieties.

THE VARIETY Symphony shows the effectiveness of achieving doubleness in the Hardy Korean type.

the moment. If in his work he brings to light one single new fact concerning the principles of plant breeding, he will have made a contribution that will be permanently valuable, and his name should go down to posterity.

It is an absolute fact—successful contradiction of which I defy—that the great names which have flashed across the horticultural firmament, the names that you conjure up when the subject of plant breeding is discussed (including that of the illustrious Burbank) are those of men who have left little in the way of permanent knowledge in connection with plant breeding. This is because they were primarily concerned with the production of new varieties. None have contributed much to the science of plant breeding. Assuredly, they should be given credit for the new things they have contributed to our gardens, but let us realize that in doing so they were too occupied to bring to light the scientific facts which are of value for all time. The science of plant breeding requires a deeper knowledge, the training and—equally important—the temperament and mental equipment of the scientist. Let the amateur and commercial breeder then be content to keep within his sphere, which is the origination of better varieties, taking advantage of the contributions of the scientist.

It has been brought to my attention by more than one discerning individual that plant breeders have been known to develop eccentricities. Looking over the field I cannot avoid this thought in spite of its prophetic undertone. While it is conceded that the plant breeder is often confronted with perplexities, there is no good reason why mental aberrations should be involved if the operator will realize his limitations and keep out of the "pseudoscientific circle." Perhaps plant breeding is so tremendously absorbing and one can become so deeply enmeshed in its possibilities that practical everyday matters lose their importance; thus a delightful pursuit or hobby becomes an obsession.

Mendel's Contribution

Unquestionably the greatest single contribution to systematic plant breeding was made by Gregor J. Mendel, an Austrian monk, who gave the world the Mendel theory in 1865. Published first in 1866 in an obscure Austrian journal, it was to all intents and purposes lost until 1900. Peculiarly enough, it was then brought to light almost simultaneously by three botanists, working quite separately—Correns in Germany, De Vries in Holland, and Tschermak in Austria. Mendel, through a series of experiments on true-breeding types of peas, demonstrated that factors or characters are heritable in a fairly definite mathematical ratio; that the immediate or first-generation hybrids of two distinct species or true-breeding types will not show the characters of the two parents, nor will they be intermediate. When two of the first-generation (F_1 technically) hybrids are interbred, some of the immediate progeny (F_2) will be of hybrid type and different from either parent; the balance like one of the grandparents. Further interbreeding or selfing of these F_2 or second-generation seedlings will again, to some extent, be different from their immediate parents or grandparents. The mathematical ratio of differentials in these second-generation hybrids would be approximately one fourth resembling one grandparent, one fourth the other grandparent, and two fourths will be more or less hybrid in type; thus, the ratio 1:2:1.

Thanks to this Mendel discovery, plant breeding on a systematic basis has made rapid strides since 1900. Breeders at last knew that it was not a hit-or-miss process or one in which the magic wand had any part, but a process conforming to fairly definite laws, governing the transfer of hereditary characters. However, inasmuch as the majority of plant breeders are not working on true-breeding types or species, but rather on hybrids of decidedly mixed ancestry, the mathematical ratio will not hold. *The great truth that desired characters may not appear in a first-generation hybrid (but from the further interbreeding, or selfing the succeeding generations) is the whole basis of consistent breeding.*

It will be apparent, then, that it is desirable to know the ancestry or pedigree of parents to predict the outcome of a cross and to some extent estimate its acceptability to outside or new factors.

To the beginner in plant breeding the first requirement would be a fairly intimate knowledge of the material being used. Hence, it would be desirable as a beginner to confine your efforts to one or two groups. Cultivate an intimate knowledge of varieties available and their more distantly related types or family group.

Opportunity for Improvement

Many of our garden families are comparatively easy to hybridize. Their after requirements are so simple that no special equipment is needed other than a cold frame to start the seed and protect the seedlings in their early stages. A few are suggested here, with a hint or two as to desirable improvements:

1. The Garden Chrysanthemum. (*a*) Added hardiness. (*b*) Early-flowering varieties capable of resisting hot weather, of producing perfect early flowers, and of flowering effectively throughout the season. (The consummation of this would greatly extend the area in which garden chrysanthemums could be grown.) (*c*) A tough foliage texture to better resist insects which now badly disfigure many sorts. (*d*) A better flower substance or texture that will not be injured by early frosts. (*e*) Dwarf types suitable for edging, bordering, and the rock garden. (*f*) Larger double varieties which will respond to disbudding and resist bad weather conditions. (*g*) Added fragrance. (*h*) New solid colors or combination of colors.

142

LARGE-FLOWERED varieties of chrysanthemums make ideal
accent flowers for autumn arrangements. (Arrangement
by Mrs. John Delafield.)

F<small>EW</small> <small>PLANTS</small> in the hardy border supply such good material for "one-flower" arrangements as do the hardy mums.

2. Hardy Pinks. A more perennial type; most are biennial now. Same applies to the hardy carnation.

3. Hardy Phlox. (*a*) Large-flowering tall varieties. (*b*) Also earlier and later kinds are needed to spread the season. (*c*) Better lavender-blue and scarlet-orange colors needed.

4. Hemerocallis (daylilies). (*a*) Longer flowering period. (*b*) Perfected colors. (*c*) Larger flowering, tall types. (*d*) Additional colors.

5. Violas. More colors in the Jersey Gem type.

6. Veronica (speedwell). More colors in the giant *subsessilis* type. White, light-blue, and pink shades not available but possible.

7. Lupines. Heat-resisting type.

8. Hardy asters. (*a*) Mildew and rustproof kinds. (*b*) Better pink and red sorts.

9. Delphiniums. Endless opportunities here. Particularly needed is a type between the dwarf Chinense and the taller Belladonna for massing. This should not be too difficult.

There is no limit to the number of groups; no apparent limitation to the material from which the breeder can draw and still readily see room for further needed improvement. I think it can also be said that no one group can ever be perfected or bred to a stage where further breeding would be degenerating in effect. When any given group has been bred to this point, then Nature, incessantly seeking variation, provides a break or mutation which man can develop further, or a new species is discovered which serves the same purpose. Examples of this are found in our most favored garden subjects. For instance, the *grandiflora* type sweet pea was bred to the point where further improvement seemed improbable. Then the ruffled petal appeared as a natural mutation, furnishing the nucleus of an entirely new group with wavy petalage. Gladiolus, developed to a similar stage, was given a new impetus by use of the species *primulinus,* which added, not only delightful yellow and orange hues, but a more dainty and graceful flower spike. Fragrant species, more recently discovered, are now being used to add to the graces of this serviceable flower.

The garden rose has experienced a succession of these cyclical stages in its progressive development. The crossing of the everblooming, but tender, Tea Rose with the hardier Hybrid Perpetual (which flowered in some varieties only sporadically in autumn) gave birth to the Hybrid Tea—a group which flowers almost continually from June until the season's end, many varieties of which are on a par with the Hybrid Perpetual in point of hardiness. This Hybrid Tea group was in time developed to the stage where all the colors and good traits of its ancestors could be demonstrated in a comparatively few well-chosen kinds. Then Pernet Ducher, that outstanding breeder of roses, obviously realizing that new blood lines were needed, succceeded in establishing a cross between a Hybrid Perpetual and a Persian Yellow (the latter a stout shrub-like rose, its vivid yellow color far exceeding in brilliance the hybrid varieties then existing). Through consistent breeding practice this better yellow shade has been imparted to the Hybrid Tea group, as exemplified in Ville de Paris and Claudius Pernet. Deep-orange tones logically developed from this original infusion, also many beautiful new blends, as noted in the immensely popular Talisman rose.

Similar development occurred in the climbing rose section, with the discovery and introduction of the wild Japanese *Rosa wichuraiana*. The still popular and lovely Dorothy Perkins was the forerunner of a type with better foliage and a far greater color range than previously existed. Then the larger flowering type developed by Dr. Van Fleet—of which the variety Dr. Van Fleet is still a worthy example—came into being and is now available in several colors, including yellow varieties which are immensely superior in coloring to any of their prototypes. Efforts now are in the direction of all-summer flowering climbers—surely an ambitious goal, but progress is being made. Other ramifications within the rose family are being brought about which will ensure breeding material for the future.

The garden chrysanthemum likewise attained a development just a few years ago that apparently defied other than minor improvement. The wild species *coreanum* provided new factors which altered the whole picture to such an extent that we can feel that, rather than having attained perfection, new paths are open leading to varieties better than we now conceive.

The daylily (hemerocallis) group offers a striking example of recent breeding progress. The known history of the daylily dates back to 1570. Always a serviceable, easily grown plant, it has for centuries found a place in the garden. Going back to 1900—a very short period in view of its lengthy existence—we find just a few varieties mentioned. Since then the improvement measured in time seems almost miraculous. The names Yeld, Perry, and Farr are prominent in its sudden rise to undreamed-of popularity. It is gratifying to note that much of this recent progress has been accomplished here in the United States. Carl Betscher of Dover, Ohio, has done much in developing the daylily to a status of commercial importance by producing a group of better varieties, such as his Bay State, Anna Betscher, Cressida, J. A. Crawford, Mrs. W. H. Wyman, and numerous others, which have been instrumental in spreading the flowering season from July into September.

It is in this hemerocallis group, I believe, that we have the best demonstration of scientific and practical breeding tactics in combination. Until recently daylily colors available were yellow, orange, and the tawny crimson. Dr. Stout of the New York Botanical Garden has taken this rather unpromising material plus some European varieties and wild species from the Orient, where they have existed for centuries, and developed a range of color that would have been simply inconceivable twenty-five years ago. So recent, in fact, is this development of new colors that, with pastel-pink shades on through to striking crimson and maroon colors emanating from Dr. Stout's crucible, it will be obvious that the daylily is entering a new era of usefulness.

Amateur Breeders

Mention must also be made of Franklin B. Meade, an amateur breeder who produced, among other fine new hemerocallis, Hyperion, a variety with so many good qualities I would give it *first* preference in my garden.

Amateur breeders have, in fact, brought us many of our finest garden strains. Such names as Mrs. Scott Elliott are prominent in connection with columbines, Miss Dean with hardy primroses, Robinson with hybrid pyrethrum or painted daisies.

Another recent example of amateur accomplishment is demonstrated in the development of the first true pink hardy aster of the *novae angliae* (New England) type. Perhaps because this hardy aster is a native of America, it has received scant attention from breeders here. The European specialists have brought about most of the improvement, and we eagerly import at substantial prices their better sorts.

The late Willard Harrington, Williamsburg, Iowa, loved the native aster, and grew it as a hobby. Farming being his occupation, he had little time for hybridizing. Seed was sown from native types showing variation or improvement. Selecting the choicest only for parents, a superior group was in time developed. From these one was selected and named Harrington's Pink. Inasmuch as this variety is the first true rose-pink hardy aster, its development is a worthy achievement in itself. Equally important, however, is the fact that this introduction will open the way for a new pink group of many desired shades.

BREEDING CHRYSANTHEMUMS

The Mechanics

The chrysanthemum is technically classed as a "composite." It is a complete flower, with pistils and stamens (female and male organs). It is, therefore, capable of fertilizing its own flower, and it is very apt to do so. A seedling thus produced would be technically known as a "self." Its chances of being better than the parent are too remote and hazy to interest the breeder. The crossed seedling, involving two parents and being more hybrid, should have greater virility and greater potential, if not apparent, value.

In a chrysanthemum the stamens and pistils are readily identified: as in most composites the pistils and stamens are closely associated and rather difficult to separate completely, particularly in the

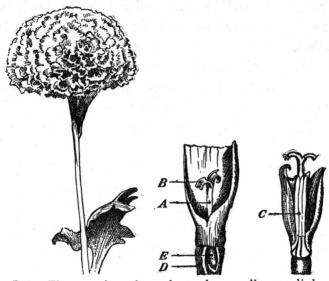

Left: Flower trimmed, ready to have pollen applied. *Center:* Ray floret, with pistillate (female) organs. *Right:* Disk floret, with staminate (male) organs also. *A,* style; *B,* stigma; *C,* stamens; *D,* ovary; *E,* seed. (From the *Chrysanthemum Manual,* by Elmer D. Smith.)

center of the flowers. There is, however, a separate pistil to be found at the base of the complete or lower petals. It is safer, then, to remove entirely the central part of the flower, and for that reason a double or semi-double flower is easier to work with. My advice to the beginner would be to get complete information as to the structure of the flower from someone who has had experience in flower breeding. Go to your state experiment station, or your state college, or to anyone who has studied plant breeding. You will find them an accommodating lot; you will be speaking their language. This will be much easier than working it out through written instructions and may prevent mistakes.

Hybridizing equipment should include:

Scissors, a pair of sharply pointed manicure ones (I prefer the slightly curved type).

Tweezers, diagonally pointed, to remove pollen sacs.

Camel's-hair brushes (several of these). A clean brush must be used for every cross. The type used for fine lettering can be had from your paint dealer.

Wax paper, either transparent or green, such as florists use. This can be cut to any size needed. Clips for same. (Cellophane retains too much moisture.)

Labels, 3½-inch painted and copper wired, secured from your seedsman or nurseryman; or strung tags, which are neater, may be obtained from your stationer.

Magnifying glass—a good pocket lens or reading glass will help in making sure that the stigmas are in a receptive stage and that the pollen adheres.

CHRYSANTHEMUM HYBRIDIZING

Best Time

Your location will be a deciding factor as to the proper time. In New England the season is too short to ripen seed out of doors successfully, except in very early varieties, and even then it is never sure. A cool greenhouse or artificial shelter and heat are necessary. From Philadelphia south much of this work can be carried on outdoors, but again the protection of sash would be desirable. Varieties that normally flower early seldom produce fertile pollen. The heat of late summer apparently militates against this. Nature seems to prescribe the cool nights of autumn as a logical time for perfect flowers. Good pollen is then available, so that the best time is just as early as there are perfect flowers.

Preparing Seed Parents

Chrysanthemums will bear seed, of course, under normal garden conditions, where the season permits. Better control is assured if the seed bearers are grown in pots. Here they can be kept a little on the dry side after the flowers commence opening, also they can be shifted around conveniently, which is often desirable. It is perfectly feasible to lift the plants from the garden just before the flowers show color and to plant them in pots or boxes just large enough to hold them comfortably. As a matter of fact, the writer has made a regular practice of lifting hybrids—flowering for the first time—after the flowers open, sometimes after they show frost injury. In spite of the mauling around and other abuses incidental to hybridizing, they will bear seed. These plants, of course, should not be overfed or overwatered at any time. Keep them on the dry side and a little hungry.

Preparing the Flower

Inasmuch as the stigma which will receive the pollen is hidden close to the base of the petal and hardly accessible, it is necessary to trim the petals back to where the stigmas can be seen. I prefer to work on a partially developed flower, trimming the petals at intervals as they mature from the base up. Within a day or two after trimming the stigmas will develop somewhat further and project sufficiently to be conveniently pollinized.

Applying the Pollen

First examine the stigmas to be sure that no foreign pollen is present. Apply the pollen with a clean brush, using a very light touch. Examination of the stigma again through a lens will indicate quickly if the pollen adheres. If not, probably the stigma has not reached the receptive stage. Save the pollen and try again the following day. Pollen carried over a few days may show a tendency to congeal. If so, place the paper unopened in a warm, sunny spot for a short time. It soon becomes workable. When the pollen supply for a particular cross is plentiful, use a comparatively large brush. Sometimes just blowing the pollen directly from the paper on to the flower head does the job satisfactorily. When just a few grains of pollen are available, a toothpick can be used rather than a brush. The operator will soon develop a technique in this work that can be acquired only from actual practice. Pollen adheres readily when the stigmas reach the receptive stage, which the operator soon learns to recognize. Four or five applications of pollen may be required to complete the cross. Pollen usually works best between 9 and 12 A.M. and on a warm, sunny day. When ripe, it can be rubbed from the anthers onto wax paper, from which the brush will take it up readily. If desirable, it can be transferred to capsules or bottles where it will keep several weeks, retaining its effectiveness. To prevent accidental pollinization, the crossed flower, also the pollen-bearing flower, should be always carefully covered. A label should be attached indicating the parents, a check mark being added with each application of pollen where many crosses are being made; thus none are overlooked. The paper covering is removed from the seed heads when the stigma matures and there is no danger of further pollinization.

POLLINATED PLANTS AND SEED—AFTERCARE

Ripening the Seed

Two or three months may be required to ripen the seed. During this period plants should be kept in a sunny, well-ventilated location, with a night temperature between 45 and 50 degrees. Day tem-

153

perature may run up to 70 degrees during sunny weather. I find that crosses made late in the season are difficult to mature successfully, because of the cloudy, cold weather prevailing at that season. Placing the plants on shelves so that the seed tops reach within a foot or so of the greenhouse heating pipes will hasten maturity and counteract the tendency to mildew from the prevailing excessive moisture.

Harvesting Seed

The stems immediately beneath the seed head will discolor and show some shrinkage by the time the seed is ready to pick. A gentle rub with the thumb will indicate the right stage, when the seed head separates at a touch. Remove the seed head with an inch or so of stem, place in small envelopes, and keep in a dry place until they are ready for cleaning, which will be two or three weeks later.

Cleaning Seed

This is an interesting winter pastime. Sometimes the formation and size of seed will convey advance information, that is, where selective or line breeding is being practiced. A simple technique requires only a flour sifter, purchased at the five-and-ten (or surreptitiously extracted from the kitchen equipment), and the lid of a shoe box. Place the screen in one end and rub the seed head until it is as fine as pipe tobacco. The seed and fine chaff will pass

154

through the screen. Then tilt the box lid slightly, tapping the underside gently. Most of the seed will promptly gravitate to the lower end. Further rubbing of the remnants plus a little judicious blowing (at which any garden enthusiast is proficient) will remove most of the chaff. Cleaned seed can be sealed in small glazed envelopes, secured from your stationer, and kept until sown in an airtight Mason jar in the electric refrigerator.

Sowing Seed

(See also Chrysanthemums from Seed, page 136.) Special cultural attention will naturally be given this blue-blooded seed, and every effort will be made to get perfect germination. The important thing being to build up strong, husky plants, there will be no harm in starting the seed somewhat earlier than generally advised. From here on the treatment will be routine. Be careful, however, at all times, when handling seed or transplanting seedlings, as to proper labeling, so that mixtures do not occur. Inaccurate pedigrees must be assiduously avoided.

BREEDING HINTS IN BRIEF

That "like begets like" is far from being true where chrysanthemum hybridizing is concerned, yet it is so to this extent: To improve a type or particular color use parents of that type or color;

thus you can best approach perfection. Crossing a red variety with a white, or a huge double flower with a tiny Pompon can only result in a miscellany of color or types that would require much further breeding to correct. Actually the selective work of previous breeders has been unscrambled here. However, as the continued interbreeding of a particular type or color goes on, there is a slowing up of the improvement. Some one factor—it may be plant vigor, foliage texture, or flower quality—may show deterioration from too close breeding. The remedy, then, would be to use another parent, not immediately related, to bring in new blood lines. For example, in the development of the single Korean Hybrid the Pompon Early Bronze was used as one parent, the other being a F_1, hybrid of *coreanum*. In this, as in almost every instance where distinctly different types are used, further interbreeding was needed to attain the desired end. From another ramification of this combination of Pompon and Single types, Indian Summer, a very double flower over 3 inches across, was produced, the variety Aladdin being the added parent. Another lead from this same combination is producing some excellent true Pompons with distinctly better colors and a more graceful branching habit, which simply demonstrates that all the types involved can be retained and improved in the process.

Having chosen, after careful deliberation, the type or types of plants on which to experiment, the next important decision would be needed improvement. If you are familiar with the material, varieties available, et cetera, and the more distantly related forms, that is an advantage. If not, that should not deter you. You will soon get acquainted. Next, realize that persistence is absolutely essential. As Mendel points out, results should not be expected in one generation. To develop any particular trait further, the first cross could not be sufficient. Crossing or selfing of further generations will be involved. It is in the juggling of the hybrids that intuition is desirable. Sometimes the poorest of these may carry the desired combination of factors, and all that is required is selfing, to produce the very thing you desire. The ability to select the potential parents at this unfinished stage, I believe, distinguishes the consistently successful breeder from the "in and outer."

Putting it another way, the successful operator develops breeding lines with the entire pedigree of which he is familiar. From trial and experiment he knows what factors his parents transmit or reproduce, and this brings up the matter of *records*.

THE IMPORTANCE OF RECORDS

Have you ever visited the experimental grounds of a seed or plant-breeding establishment? If so, then you have noticed the almost complete absence of names in the labeling of new varieties. Numbers instead, perhaps in combination with initial letters, are used. The casual visitor may conclude that these apparently meaningless characters are intended to conceal true identities or names. Usually the truth of the matter is that they have no names and, in the sequence of development, have become far removed from any named parent. Accordingly, most breeders keep careful records of every cross, also of the parentage of every seedling selected for further breeding. Those who fail to do so, devoutly wish they had. It would be exasperating to develop several fine seedlings with some cherished trait from a combination of a previous year and then not have the combination. That can easily happen. No one particular method of recording prevails. Breeders of my acquaintance adopt or develop the method that best suits their need or fancy. I would suggest the use of two books: one to record original crosses only. This in the course of time will prove valuable in preventing the repetition of a forgotten cross. Notations should be made here also on crosses that fail to click. If successful, note the general characteristics of the seedlings. The second book should be substantially bound and of compact pocket size for field reference. This is for recording pedigrees. A simple system is to number seedlings selected for further breeding in the order in which they are selected, adding the year. Thus seedling 9–37 would be the ninth seedling selected in the year 1937. Labeled thus, it is entered in the field book, noting

Eugene A. Wander, largest of early-flowering double varieties, gives the effect of a flood of golden sunshine in the border, and is a favorite for cutting.

BRONZE SPOON IS a pleasing color in this group, all of
which have become great favorites with flower arrangers.

parentage, flowering date, color, size, growing habit, and character variations.

Each year starts a new number series; thus, by referring back from parent to parent, the complete ancestry is readily available. Selfing or inbreeding is an important angle in plant development. The progeny from seedling 9–37 would be labeled 9–37 F_1, and the progeny of these seedlings would in turn be 9–37F_2. The letter "F" is the accepted symbol for "filial descendant." Certain seedlings might be chosen from 9–37 progeny to be used for further breeding or for possible introduction. These should have individual identification. As they would be selected the next year, the number series would begin 1–38—parentage and descriptive matter then following. It is obvious that the records of a few years of plant breeding will quickly indicate the best parents. Details are easily forgotten. As a case in point, the unusual size of the fine chrysanthemum Granny Scovill was an unexpected development. The immediate parents were known as carrying the factors for good bronze colors. Traced back, it developed that a great grandparent was a large greenhouse variety, discontinued because it did not appear to be desirable. Its influence was felt several generations away, and as a consequence this forgotten parent was used again and is partially responsible for a fine breeding line of double Korean Hybrids.

HARDY CHRYSANTHEMUMS

MUTATIONS
The Unlike

Herein lies the "spice" of a captivating hobby. It is another manifestation of Nature's ceaseless effort to provide variety. Nowhere is it so apparent as in artificially bred hybrids where an added irritant is present. Surprises are not uncommon, and sometimes the unlooked-for product is far more thrilling than the expected. New leads are thus established for the breeder to use to advantage.

The writer's experience with *Chrysanthemum arcticum* nicely illustrates Nature's capriciousness. Some ten years of breeding effort with *arcticum,* attempting to combine its extreme hardiness with the desirable traits of several garden varieties, have not materialized a first-class hybrid, although thousands of seedlings have been raised and no promising combination or recombination has been overlooked. *Arcticum* normally breeds true to type. Recently in Pennsylvania a lovely pink hybrid appeared in a batch of the typical variety. Whether a seedling or a sport (mutation), the fact remains that the first and only hybrid of *arcticum* disseminated was supplied by sheer accident. It is now named Astrid—a lovely worth-while addition.

It is interesting to note here that the originators of Astrid—Mr. and Mrs. J. Franklin Styer, Concordsville, Pennsylvania—have developed a new group of single varieties not unlike the Korean Hybrids in color, but with longer petals. The foliage and growing habit are like those of *arcticum,* and the group which carries the extreme hardiness of this grandparent has been appropriately named Northland Daisies.

Mr. Styer informs me that Astrid itself failed to produce worth-while seedlings. This breakup occurred in a second generation grown from seed taken from a group of field plants. Here is a striking instance of mutation. Doubtless a single plant of Astrid developed the gene combination from which this distinct and no doubt valuable new type materialized. Mother Nature, in this instance, made possible the consummation of an objective which the writer failed to attain in many years of intensive breeding. Mr. and Mrs. Styer are commended for their persistence and good judgment in taking advantage of an unusual opportunity.

Gypsophila "Bristol Fairy"

Leaving chrysanthemums for the moment, we find a more fruitful example in the Double Babysbreath Bristol Fairy, originated by the writer. Although produced under more or less artificial manipulation, the variety was far beyond the original conception, which was simply a cleaner white, earlier-flowering form of the old double paniculata florepleno. Were it possible to impart the thrill, the excitement, and the mixed anticipation (and apprehension) incidental to its complete development in that first year or two, while it was under trial, it would be easily understood why plant breeding is a captivating hobby.

Its development began with a seedling from the original double form, which differed only in that the plant was more loose jointed, the semi-double flower a somewhat cleaner white than the type. The seeds, which are not produced freely, were carefully hand-picked, stored until February, then started under glass. Two years elapsed before they flowered. Seed was taken again from the most promising, and two years later over a thousand plants of this, the third generation, were in flower. True to form, the first to bloom were single, as was expected. Some two weeks later the first double forms appeared.

The big moment had arrived. Each morning the plants were inspected carefully. They proved disappointing as they developed, mostly dirty white, some double to the point of malformation; none so far worth the effort.

Then a plant was noted—because the flowers were really white and larger than the type, the growth more luxuriant, *but* the flowers, widely spaced, developed a scant-appearing spray. So far the plant was of interest only because it was different. It might produce seed and thus lead to something better. "Just a potential breeder." The plant was accordingly staked and labeled. With the end of the flowering season, early August, no further

DEAN KAY, a deep pink, has larger flowers than Amelia or Azaleamum, and is one of the hardiest of the "cushions."

MARJORIE MILLS, very dwarf and compact in habit, rich
autumn red in color, is perfect for a low informal border.

attention was indicated for these gypsophilas until seed would ripen.

With the multiplicity of other small details, little heed was paid to this unpromising experiment. Passing this spot during the cool of a September evening, a fairly substantial mass of white was noticed well up in one of the rows among the maturing seed branches. The immediate reaction, "Well! how come boneset among those gyps? Careless weeding by someone!" A second look in the dimming twilight excited curiosity. "But boneset wouldn't look just like that!" Approaching the plant with increasing trepidation, the question in mind, "Is it a babysbreath? No, it couldn't be at this season. But it is! and an entirely different one." Pure-white flowers, still too widely spaced, but a real second crop; husky lateral branches from the base of the plant, promising still more. Well, this was something different. No other variety of gypsophila flowered more than once, or as late in the season. *It was a find!* Before the summer ended some forty cuttings were taken, and the peculiar circumstance here was that thirty-five of these rooted—a far better batting average than has ever been attained since, in spite of more concentrated effort on its propagation. Grafting, the usual procedure for Double Babysbreath, was, of course, resorted to, and from then on increase was rapid. Introduced in 1927, its acceptance was universal. This original plant has since then multiplied to quantities far exceeding the million mark.

It might be an interesting breeding note to point out that Bristol Fairy does not produce seed, nor could it be made to do so by resorting to any of the usual aids such as restricting the roots in pots, withholding water when in flower, or crippling the growth in other ways. From some young plants subjected to X-ray treatment (2400 units), a few seeds were secured in spite of the fact that this treatment induces sterility as a rule. Three plants were flowered, all of which were of the original single *paniculata* type. Another generation of these to flower next summer may produce the hoped-for varieties. Judging by foliage and general growing habit, however, they are of the *paniculata* type. Inasmuch as Bristol Fairy was under suspicion of having some *acutifolia*—which it resembles most closely—in its make-up, these grandchildren prove rather conclusively that its wide difference must be attributed to Nature's mutational proclivities, rather than to some philandering vegetative iceman.

Accidents of Nature

It is well known that nearly all table varieties of apples are of accidental origin. Another example of Nature's handiwork is found in the famous Temple orange. Far more delicious than any man-made variety, it is by origin a wildling, as was the seedless or Washington Navel variety. Examples, in fact, are to be seen everywhere among our plant acquaintances. The point for the experimenter to keep in mind is that Nature can forever excel his efforts, but she also can and will render assistance. Keep this in mind when you arrive at that discouraged stage when you might conclude that the whole business of plant breeding is perhaps chimerical. I doubt if any embryonic plant experimenter has escaped this faltering stage. That is the time to tighten your belt, elevate your chin, and go to it with added faith.

CHAPTER VIII

REMINISCING

KOREAN HYBRID CHRYSANTHEMUM TYPE

Its Development in Detail

THE conception and development of the Korean Hybrid type resulted from a stubborn belief that hardier and better garden chrysanthemums could be developed; the pursuit of that belief has blazed the trail whose end is not yet but is, let us hope, still in the distance. I can say with assurance that these Korean Hybrids are but a beacon to mark the way and that better chrysanthemums in new types and varieties are in the offing. The inspiration for this particular endeavor may be traced to a genuine admiration for a plant of such serviceable character. Nor was its brave effort to embellish our gardens, when all other bloom had passed, without direct appeal, also.

New England conditions are notoriously temperamental and difficult for late-flowering subjects. Its first frosts destroying the average plants are normally followed by weeks of autumnal weather with the glorious foliage colors of the Indian summer. Providing they escaped this severe frost, the comparatively few chrysanthemums available, which were early enough in flowering to span this period, were limited in color range, also in their ability to stand the rigors of the winter. Vying with these were the hardy but extremely late bloomers of older vintage. Such kinds as Normandie, Yellow Normandie, Perle Chatillonaise, Alice Howell, Ruth Cumming, and Glory of Seven Oaks were leading the procession in 1920, remarkably large quantities of them being purchased each season, which indicated a wide interest in the earlier type as a garden subject, in spite of their lack of sturdiness. The problem, then, was to develop more varieties which would flower early, to increase the color range, and to add a greater degree of hardiness; to combine, in fact, the best traits of the available kinds. Accordingly, a search began for those sorts which had survived a number of seasons under severe garden conditions. The farmhouses and hills of Connecticut proved a happy hunting ground. Among those procured, which were actually few in number, none promised much in the way of color betterment, but some did promise additional hardiness. Among these, the old magenta-pink variety Autumn Glow was contributed by Miss Nellie Minor, a neighbor, whose garden, high on the crest of Chippens Hill, encounters everything that a Connecticut winter provides. Through the years these plants had acquired hardiness to an unusual degree.

The breeding chart on page 185 indicates the particular stage, where Barbara Cumming—early flowering—the seed bearer or mother plant, was crossed with Autumn Glow, late and hardy. Following the chart down, it will be seen that seedling 3-29, later named Ruth Hatton, arrived two generations afterward. Other varieties appeared also in this generation, including Jean Treadway, October Girl, Jean Cumming, and Daybreak, some of which were better adapted to our garden conditions and all desirable in some respect. A halt was evident at this stage, because further interbreeding, while developing other worth-while varieties, added nothing to the hardiness. Good additions came more reluctantly, the group in effect having been rather thoroughly explored. Since necessity is the mother of invention, it appeared that the answer would be in new and more virile blood, which meant the introduction of some entirely distinct but related species. It was anticipated that the blending of a wild species with the cultivated group would involve lengthy manipulation before desirable results could be obtained. It was the only course to pursue, however, so an exploration of the numerous relatives got under way. The species *coreanum,* although introduced from Korea some time previously, was not in garden usage. It was first brought to the public attention by Harlan P.

Kelsey, who was captivated by the lovely chasteness and charm peculiar to this wildling. The extreme hardiness and vigorous habit of growth attracted my attention. These were needed traits. Reference to the chart will show where a cross between *coreanum* and Ruth Hatton was obtained. At the same time a reverse cross was made, as well as several others. Ruth Hatton, always a noble parent, however, blazed the trail for remarkable developments, because nearly all the Korean Hybrids today came through, and from, this particular combination.

Just by way of illustrating the procedure involved in developing worth-while varieties from a species-hybrid cross, I will, at the risk of boring the reader, cite a few of the early details, for they were replete with thrills from the first indication that a cross had been established and on through the succeeding generations, each a step along the way, until the final development of hybrids worthy of the name.

I clearly recollect the making of the original Ruth Hatton *coreanum* cross, and for some indefinable reason I had the feeling that the combination was a logical one. The cross was made in October 1928. Some thirty seedlings, of those procured, flowered in the fall of 1929. None of these, casually inspected, appeared different from an adjoining group of Ruth Hatton selfed seedlings. At this particular stage, however, the breeder cannot be casual in checking possible hybrids. If a single seedling shows the slightest trace of its two parents, then its potential merit is established, whether it is attractive in itself or so lacking in merit that an immediate ride to the rubbish heap is indicated. There is absolute truth in the familiar adage "Beauty is only skin deep." It goes without saying that these thirty-odd seedlings were inspected most thoroughly from day to day. Soon one plant, still in tight bud, was selected because it had a rather odd and rugged type of growth. The flower buds were arranged in a peculiar spiral or candelabrumlike spray that was not characteristic of a Ruth Hatton or any *hortorum* seedling. Also there was something different in its general appearance, too insignificant actually to identify, but undeniable nevertheless—perhaps it was just a lucky hunch. The plant was lifted, carefully boxed, and brought under glass for further observation. With the opening of the flowers, the characteristics of the seedling became tremendously interesting; the flowers, odd in their cup formation, developed two to four rows of uneven, ragged petals, with one highly exciting trait. They were a purer white than any seedling that I had ever seen, with a substance and gloss that positively indicated the Korean parent. The central stamens and pistils were badly disarranged and the stigma carried an unusual blotched effect in the recurving surface. Regardless of its "Raggedy Ann" appearance, the important fact was apparent that it

SEPTEMBER GOLD is a cushion-type pompon making
rounded plants. Charming for cutting, too.

SEPTEMBER CLOUD (*right*) and SEPTEMBER BRONZE are companions to September Gold— a trio of early dwarf pompons.

positively indicated the Korean parent. This was the fact that I was anxious to establish, because there is always the possibility that the affinity necessary for the combination may not have existed. This is only too apt to occur when species blood is being introduced.

Labeled and identified as seedling 64-29 this first hybrid became one of the progenitors of the many named hybrids now in general use. It is regrettable now that this hybrid connecting link was not retained as a matter of sentiment.

A fact of some significance from a genetical viewpoint, if from no other, may be worth pointing out here. Since the known history of the chrysanthemum, which dates back to the period 550 B.C., only two species, *indicum* and *morifolium*—if we assume these to be true species—have been involved in the development of the garden chrysanthemum. There is not a single indication that another species was used to any purpose in a period of over two thousand years, until October 1928, when this *coreanum* Ruth Hatton cross was effected. This is an astonishing fact in view of the long and concerted efforts being made in the breeding of hardy chrysanthemums. The citation of the fact is to call attention to the unusual circumstances rather than to boast of an accomplishment. The simple truth is that *Chrysanthemum coreanum* is a receptive and pliant species. Garden cultivation in due time would have produced a similar range of hybrids. It just happened to be my good fortune to stumble across this valuable parent before it was discovered by some other breeder.

From the original cross the further development shown on the chart is a matter of actual record. It is hoped that its presentation in this form may be of value to the tyro in plant breeding and of possible interest to the more experienced breeder. Before leaving the subject I would call attention to another interesting genetical aspect, the true solution of which I cheerfully leave to someone with a more scientific background. *Coreanum,* white, breeds true to type from seed, but when blended with Ruth Hatton, it has brought to us many lovely tints and color combinations that did not previously exist. The direct progeny of Ruth Hatton, when selfed, produces the customary colors of the older *hortorum* types. How can we account for this new color range? What impressed me as being a logical answer was brought to my attention by Mrs. J. A. Vanderpoel—a most remarkable lady now in her nineties, but with a degree of mental agility that would shame the average youngster. Her lifelong training in the art of color manipulation and a wide knowledge of pigmentation aroused her curiosity in the problem. Mrs. J. A. Vanderpoel advances the theory that no actual new color factor has been added but that the petal surface of *coreanum,* which is starch-like and glossy, elaborates existing colors through greater reflection, just as the surface of a color-film screen may affect the reproduced picture.

INTRODUCING A NEW CHRYSANTHEMUM

Before the "subdebutante" arrives at the coming-out stage and is ready to make her bow with the annual influx of novelties for the acceptance of the great gardening public, there is a lengthy period of preparation and grooming. More detail and expense are involved than one might suppose. First of all, the producer who can consistently select five new varieties from an average annual output of ten thousand cross-numbered seedlings is doing well. If he greatly exceeds this quantity, he is either endowed with unusual breeding skill or with a lack of conscience, either of which may be profitable assets.

From the day a seedling is selected for the grooming referred to previously until it appears in the catalogues at least three years of testing will have passed. That would be the shortest possible period. The first year is well past before a desirable variety is selected for trial. In the second season ten to twenty-five plants raised from the original are grown and during the flowering stage are accurately checked. If the variety lives up to its early qualifications, one half of the plants are left out in the open ground to be tested for winter hardiness; the balance are brought in under glass for further propagation, and from these, possibly one hundred and fifty cuttings are rooted. If the outside plants, under average winter conditions, show sufficient hardiness, well and good. The one hundred and fifty cuttings are planted out for further checking. The outside plants in autumn will indicate the behavior of the variety in the two-year stage. In the meantime, growing habits and resistance to disease in hot weather are to be considered, also the behavior of the variety under fair—rather than good—cultural conditions, for it is the former with which the average plant must contend. Briefly, it must be reasonably foolproof. Thus the second year is passed. Assuming that no weakness or fault has developed and, of course, that the variety has the necessary distinctiveness and charm, then from the plants on hand it should be possible to produce between seven and ten thousand young plants ready for sale the following spring, provided that the variety is prolific in its stooling or suckering habit. Many kinds are not—a bad omen, for the absence of these bottom growths usually indicates lack of hardiness. In spite of the perfect performance covering this three-year period, there is still a possibility that some kink or fault may come to the surface, so the careful producer insists on another year for rechecking—a sort of postgraduate course. Let it be said here that the introducer as a rule will not deliberately foist an unworthy variety on the long-suffering plant buyer. Not that he is saturated with the honesty and virtue supposedly acquired through

DWARF IN HABIT, and one of the earliest of all pompons, is Pygmy Gold, with open sprays of small golden flowers.

RICHEST IN color of all the pompons is Ruby Pompon,
with cupped petals that make it unusually interesting.

close contact with the soil, the flowers, and all that is beautiful in nature, but because it "just isn't good business." Anyone with intelligence enough to produce new varieties should have horse sense enough to realize this truth, but failing in that, then the matter of paternal pride should still prevail. There is, of course, always the opportunist who can high-pressure a mediocre novelty into half the gardens of the nation and profit mightily in so doing. Through the influence of the many well-organized garden clubs and the fine educational features of the garden magazines, the horticulturally minded public is too well informed to be swindled more than once by this sort of individual.

I have indicated that five good new varieties from ten thousand plants is a good "batting average," also the quantities needed for testing and propagation. It is likely, however, that twenty white hopes were selected to obtain, through devious elimination, the five in question. Not infrequently these discards may have been carried through the second and third year. With the propagation entailed it will be apparent that several thousand plants are also grown and destroyed. For that reason, a good novelty is worth the price asked for it, and, in paying it, the purchaser is contributing his, or more likely her, share toward that horticultural progress he or she above all desires.

What's in a Name?

A good name has a very distinct bearing on the career of a new garden aspirant. One that is cumbersome or that is lacking in appeal is forever a detriment, no matter how good the variety. That is why European varieties, particularly those of roses, with lengthy, unpronounceable names are often renamed before they are accepted here. This practice, hardly justified even in the interest of a deserving variety, is generally frowned on. Neither the American Rose Society nor the Chrysanthemum Society of America will officially recognize varieties so named. Incidentally, renaming is not by any means a recent evil. Chrysanthemum growers of almost a century ago could give the present generation valuable pointers in this matter. Payne, in his remarkable little book *The History of the Chrysanthemum,* gives a list of over fifty varieties, mostly of French origin, with synonyms, mainly English. This was about the year 1850.

Undoubtedly a name short and descriptive, one that breathes a promise of some alluring trait or quality, is the perfect name. It intrigues.

Where chrysanthemums are concerned, a name should be submitted first to the Chrysanthemum Society of America for registration, so that duplication will not occur. Should you in a moment of inspiration find that short but apt name exactly fitting your bronze seedling, do not be surprised to find that someone has anticipated you. There is, after all, a limit to descriptive names. One of our most active introducers finds it necessary to coin hybrid or assembled names that carry no apparent meaning but do serve for identification purposes.

In naming a variety after an individual, two motives may be involved—that of basking in the reflected glory of a prominent name or, as is more often the case, a genuine desire to honor some worthy person, usually one with horticultural leanings. Circumstances connected with names may in some instances prove of interest.

The variety Granny Scovill I named for Mrs. E. H. Scovill, who, at considerable expense, maintained a lovely old-fashioned hillside garden literally teeming with color, and so located that the many passers-by could enjoy it. A broad vista was kept open with this in mind. (The customary practice is that of seclusion.) Mrs. Scovill's instructions to John, her gardener, were that the garden is always open to anyone who loves flowers. He was commissioned to make such a person welcome and let no one leave without an armful of flowers, which in my opinion is a classic example of the true spirit of gardening.

But why "Granny Scovill," you may wonder? Well, during the hectic period of the world war this lady quietly devoted all of her time and a great deal of her resources, sacrificing much, to provide the boys "over there" and here with many comforts.

Many a veteran will link with the name "Granny Scovill" numerous acts of thoughtful kindness which tended to make his tasks less arduous. Though the name "Mrs. E. H. Scovill" was of considerable social significance, it would possibly be unknown to the boys, so the variety was duly christened "Granny Scovill." It will be agreed, I feel sure, that such a person fully deserves the implied compliment, nor should it be difficult to understand why some years passed before a variety of sufficient merit was developed to bear such a worthy name.

Originators of new varieties are prone to name varieties for members of their immediate family or for themselves. This is something I would rather not do, and in view of the fact that there are three Cumming varieties, some explanation will be in order. Ruth Cumming, the first of the trio, was so named for my eldest daughter, by A. N. Pierson & Company, Cromwell, Connecticut, for whom I had done some chrysanthemum breeding. With two more envious daughters following shortly, if peace was to prevail in the Cumming clan, there was no alternative, so in time Barbara and Jean were duly added to the roster.

Nancy Copeland was named for the charming daughter of Mr. and Mrs. Harold C. Copeland, by way of appreciation for the multitude of helpful suggestions these good gardeners have contributed in connection with new varieties. This splendid chrysanthemum, grown under trial long before it

A PERKY LITTLE fall-tinted bronze is Goblin, which forms
nice open sprays for cutting and also makes a bright note
in the flower border.

JUDITH ANDERSON, a pure yellow "button" pompon, has long been popular both for garden display and for cutting.

attained a name, impressed the Copelands so emphatically that their insistence was largely responsible for this introduction.

The first of the Korean Hybrids were named
with group association in mind because the several
varieties ready for introduction represented a distinct type. Hence, ancient lore was delved into and
mythical characters appropriated. The gods and
goddesses were invoked. The significance of the
names in many instances is reasonably appropri-
ate. Mercury, messenger of the gods, was the first
Korean Hybrid, and was so named because it was
the bearer of tidings. Others would follow. Ceres,
goddess of grain, flowering in the mellow October
sunlight, leads one's thoughts to the color of a field
of ripening grain. Mars, god of war, aptly identi-
fies its blood-red namesake. Apollo, exponent of
manly beauty, is reflected in a striking color combination of lively bronzes—a man's color.

Not all names could be so appropriately placed,
but the purpose in mind was carried out. Other
breeders following suit, the gamut of these gods was
soon exhausted, and it was desirable to return to
more earthly titles.

Often some characteristic in a variety is sugges-
tive: Ember by the soft glow noticeable in its flower
in the afternoon sunshine. The Urchin, a nonde-
script waiflike type in flower, with a homely
appeal, nevertheless, was first named "Raggedy
Ann," but it was soon discovered that the "Hatton

person," mentioned below, had already applied it to one of his own orphans.

Another introducer has had excellent results in checking the immediate reaction of visitors looking over his pets. An ejaculation or first comment has furnished names altogether fitting. Again, events are sometimes so commemorated, as, for instance, in the Peony Triomphe de l'Exposition d'Lille. Lovely as it is, the handicap was too great for it to attain the popularity it fully deserves.

The greatest evil to my mind in connection with naming is the fairly frequent usage of superlatives —Very Best, Climax, "Somebody's" Perfection— or something suggesting that the ultimate has actually arrived. It never does.

The chrysanthemums Ruth and R. Marion Hatton bring to mind an amusing incident which developed later into a most cherished friendship. In browsing through *Horticulture* some years ago I became interested in an article on hardy chrysanthemums, quickly getting the impression that the author knew the varieties concerned intimately and wrote from a most sensible viewpoint. Perhaps the fact that Ruth Cumming was specified as the best all-round garden variety may have influenced me. Anyway, I wrote the author, with a complimentary reference to the article in question, which was altogether justified, extending at the same time an invitation to come to Bristol and see the seedling chrysanthemums. Thoughtlessly assuming Marion

Hatton to be a "Miss," a rather prim, precise, elderly little lady was envisioned, as is one's wont. Some correspondence ensued, the gist of which, plus a rather delicate handwriting, conveyed the idea that the little lady I had imagined also had a considerable sense of humor. "She" had. Shortly after, on a Sunday morning, the bell rang very, very early. Answering, doubtless sleepy-eyed, and wondering just what brand of pest could be so heartless as to disturb the peace and quiet of the early Sabbath, I was considerably disconcerted when the athletic-looking six-foot-two giant looming up in the doorway quietly announced himself as "Marion Hatton." The sense of humor deduction, however, was justified. It accounts for the fact that I was not put right in the matter of gender in the first place and for many amusing incidents since. Keenly analytical and practical in observing plant values, Mrs. Ruth and Mr. R. Marion have assisted and encouraged me greatly in the development and selection of varieties, so I take considerable satisfaction in the two honest and delightfully unpretentious varieties which were appropriately selected to carry their names.

This brings to mind a delightful experience that may be the lot of any dabbler in plant breeding. Traveling through Maryland early one November a chrysanthemum was noted profusely planted around a home of humble aspect. The rich, glistening yellow color, combined with the healthy, fulsome plants, indicated an unknown kind, so fine as to warrant an investigation. Answering my knock at the door, the good housewife, active in the preparation of dinner, judging by her rather determined expression, evidently assumed that it was a visit from the Fuller Brush man and didn't exactly welcome the intrusion at that busy moment.

I apologized for my badly timed visit and stated the purpose of it, which was merely to find out the name of the gorgeous yellow chrysanthemum which had captured her fancy to the exclusion of all others and to learn by what secret process such manifestly good culture was attained. Almost magically the good lady's attitude changed. The apron was whisked off and nothing short of a trip around the cottage yard would do. Closer inspection revealed that the chrysanthemum in question was none other than R. Marion Hatton, which I had originated, but failed to recognize under such superb finish, all of which added a touch of humor to the situation. Possibly the fact that the owner raised poultry and knew the virtue of poultry manure may have been partly responsible for the unusual showing this variety made. Perhaps, also, the soil or some local condition was particularly to its liking, for it was obvious that my hostess had little time to fuss with her plants. They just grew. Anyway, I have not seen such perfection since. It was fortunate that time was pressing, so this most pleasant visit was terminated as quickly as politeness dictated, for an odor of burning vegetables was distinctly noted when farewell greetings were exchanged.

If in reciting this incident as an example of that kinship, previously referred to, which prevails among plant lovers, I have taken the Fuller Brush man's name in vain, let him in return benefit by the tip herein available; and if the lady, whose name I have lost, reading these lines, recalls this visit and will supply this information, I shall be glad to renew a delightful acquaintance.

PEDIGREE CHART OF THE SINGLE KOREAN
HYBRID CHRYSANTHEMUMS

The chart shows the process followed in the development of the Korean Hybrid type, some varieties of which are omitted in the interest of simplification. It will be seen that two breeding lines are used. Reading down from the top left, Autumn Glow × Barbara Cumming starts one line; on the right, Ruth Cumming × Wells' Excelsior heads the second. Note where *coreanum* enters each group, also the fusion of the two groups, with the union of 1-31 K.C. × 5-30 K.C. The deep-red color of Mars and the salmon-red of Mercury, traceable to Gypsy Girl and Grenadier, indicate the manner in which color or other characteristics are frequently carried as a hidden recessive trait through several generations to appear again, not as before, but occasionally accented and glorified.

Brief Description of Parents Involved

Autumn Glow. Single. Magenta-pink. Very hardy. Late.

Barbara Cumming. Double. Bronze-yellow. Very early.

Normandie. Double. White. Very early. Not hardy.

Bronze Seedling. Single. Bronze-yellow. Hardy.

Coreanum. Single. White. Very hardy.

Ruth Hatton. Double. White. Early.

3-30 K.C. Single. Light yellow.

1-31 K.C. Single. Bronze-red.

Ruth Cumming. Double. Terra cotta.

Wells' Excelsior. Double. Yellow. Late.

Gypsy Girl. Single. Deep red.

Grenadier. Single. Crimson-bronze. Early.

68-29. Single. Crimson-bronze. Early.

5-30 K.C. Single. Bronze-yellow. Early.

16-31 K.C. Single. Luminous bronze. Growth poor.

15-31 K.C. Single. Tawny copper. Growth good. Very hardy.

Mercury: Single. Salmon-red. Hardy. Early.

Early Bronze. Pompon. Double. Bronze. Very early. Hardy.

PEDIGREE CHART OF THE DOUBLE KOREAN HYBRIDS

The process followed in the development of this group differs from the single Korean Hybrid group

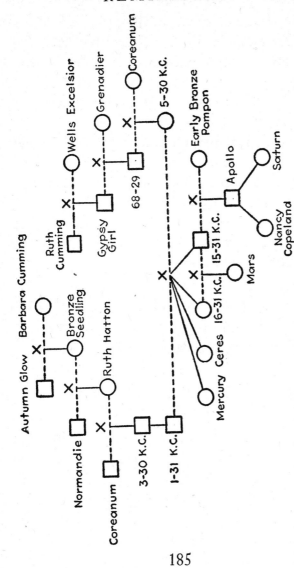

Rectangles indicate mother plants.
Circles indicate the male or pollen parent.
Each horizontal line represents a new generation, usually completed in one year.

185

largely in the selection of seedling parents showing a tendency toward doubling. Note that Mrs. Phil Page contributed to some extent its early tendency and its doubling but none of its lack of hardiness. King Midas and other varieties not shown here stemmed from this same breeding line.

Progress is being made toward increased hardiness and resistance to winter moisture through breeding these double Korean Hybrids with some of the real old-fashioned sturdy late-flowering *hortorum* varieties. New colors and blends, also earliness in flowering, are being added through the use of hybrids of related species.

Brief Description of Parents Involved

Ruth Hatton. Double. White. Early.

Coreanum. Single. White. Very hardy.

64-29. Semi-double. White tinted pink. Malformed flowers.

8-30 C.K. Semi-double. White, glossy petals. Slight malformation.

9-30 C.K. Single. White tinted pink. Glossy petals.

27-31 C.K. Semi-double. Soft biscuit yellow. Hybrid growth.

36-32 C.K. Semi-double. Lavender-pink. Vigorous hybrid habit.

Mrs. Phil Page. Double. Bronze-red. Very early. Not hardy.

UNEXCELLED for a long border or a low hedge is North Star, exceptionally hardy, and early flowering.

RICH FAWN, with a flush of salmon, Mrs. Pierre S. du-Pont, III, ranks as one of the most glamorous of all mums.

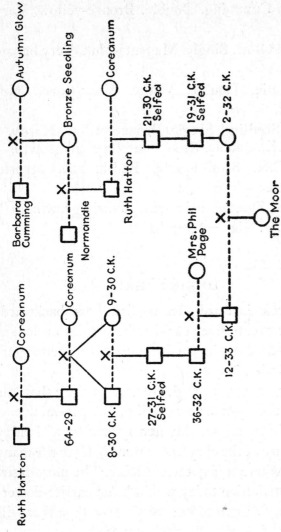

Rectangles indicate mother plants.
Circles indicate the male or pollen parent.
Each horizontal line represents a new generation, usually completed in one year.

Barbara Cumming. Double. Bronze-yellow. Very early.

Autumn Glow. Single. Magenta-pink. Very hardy. Late.

Normandie. Double. White. Very early. Not hardy.

Bronze Seedling. Single. Bronze-yellow. Hardy.

21-30 C.K. Double. Bronze-red. Hybrid growth.

19-31 C.K. Semi-double. Red-bronze. Hybrid growth.

2-32 C.K. Double. Wine-red. Hybrid growth.

The Moor. Rich amaranth.

LOOKING AHEAD

To look forward—let us first look backward. The last twenty-five years has been a revolutionary period—an era—in the development of better garden varieties.

There is not a single reason to feel that the coming twenty-five years will not be productive of better kinds and possibly new types that will carry the culture of the chrysanthemum far into the many regions where it is not now usable. The most desirable contribution today would be an earlier-flowering type, resistant to hot weather—a type that will stand wet feet as well as subzero temperatures.

Having attained a stage where the amateur finds it workable, with commercial breeding interest growing rapidly, and with vastly better material to work with, that type will surely come. The garden chrysanthemum, pliable and responsive in the breeder's hands, rather than having attained perfection, is just on the way.

CHAPTER IX

RECOMMENDED VARIETIES

A LIMITED NUMBER of varieties are suggested here to cover the complete season. They are generally satisfactory through northeastern America and, therefore, desirable in the more temperate regions where chrysanthemums can be grown. With many to choose from, it is obvious that some old favorites will be omitted, the intent being simply to bring to attention the more recent kinds and a few older ones that, in some respect, are outstanding. It will be obvious also that, with the present rapid introduction of new sorts, some of those suggested here may be quickly superseded.

SINGLE-FLOWERED

The single-flowered hardy mums, with their masses of flowers and general prolonged season of bloom, are often chosen for landscape effects where a solid mass of color is the end desired. Many gardeners like them, too, as cut flowers, especially

BURMA, VIGOROUS in growth and profuse in bloom, is a
rich glistening bronze coming in late September.

EXTRA HARDY, and unexcelled for richness and brilliancy of coloring among the copper and terra-cotta varieties, is the new mum Fred Rockwell.

when taken in large sprays. Their simplicity, particularly in arrangements with other flowers, lends a charm of naturalness that the more sophisticated double blooms cannot contribute.

Apollo. Sparkling bronze; October 5; 2½ feet.

Astrid. Soft rose; very hardy; October 5; 1½ to 2 feet.

Ceres. Tints of gold and copper; October 10; 2½ feet.

Crimson Splendor. Rich crimson; late September; 2½ feet.

Daphne. Old rose; October 10; 2½ feet.

Dubonnet. Amaranth-pink; very hardy; October 10; 2 feet.

Good Morning. Soft creamy yellow; very hardy; October 5; 1½ to 2 feet.

North Star. Glistening white; very hardy; September 20; 2½ feet.

Sappho. Pure yellow; September 20; 2 feet.

Venus. Orchid Pink; September 20; 2½ to 3 feet.

DUPLEX-FLOWERED

The duplex or semi-double-flowered mums have two or more rows of petals, but are still sufficiently open to show the contrasting center or "eye" of the flower. They combine, in a way, the charm of the simplicity of the singles and the greater substance of the fully double or decorative types. For variety's sake, a few may well be included in every garden.

191

Algonquin. Bright yellow; very hardy; September 5; 2 to 2½ feet.

Arctic Queen. Bronze salmon; very hardy; October 10; 1½ feet.

Autumn Lights. Glistening coppery bronze; very hardy; September 25; 2 feet.

Chippewa. Aster purple; September 15; 2 feet.

Fireglow. Chinese red; very hardy; September 15; 2 feet.

Louise Schling. Glowing salmon-red; October 1; 2½ feet.

Manantico. Bright red; September 15; 2½ feet.

Silver Moon. Silvery white; September 15; 2½ feet.

DOUBLE-FLOWERED

The large-flowered, fully double or "decorative" type represents the peak of achievement to date in the development of hardy garden mums. The blooms of many of these compare not unfavorably with florists' or greenhouse varieties, even when allowed to grow naturally, and if disbudded (as they can be in the open garden) reach even greater size. They make a fine show in the mixed border, and are especially desirable for cutting, particularly for arrangements, or bouquets of only one kind of flower, with or without evergreen or autumn foliage.

Avalanche. Creamy white to pure white; September 25; 2 feet.

Barbara Cumming. Yellow-bronze tinted; September 5; 1½ feet.

Burgundy. Wine red; October 5; 2½ feet.

Burma. Soft orange-bronze; September 25; 2 feet.

Cydonia. Fiery orange-bronze; October 15; 2 feet.

Early Joan Helen. Garnet shaded purple; early October; 1½ feet.

Eugene A. Wander. Golden yellow, bronze tints; September 10; 1½ feet.

King Midas. Bronze-yellow; September 20; 2 feet.

Lavender Lady. Lavender-tinted pink; October 1; 2½ feet.

Magnolia. Soft pink and yellow; very hardy; September 25; 2 feet.

Mrs. Pierre S. duPont, III. Salmon-bronze; October 5; 2½ feet.

Pink Radiance. Soft, luminous pink; very hardy; October 1; 2½ feet.

Red Velvet. Velvet crimson; very hardy; October 10; 2 feet.

Rose Glow. Raspberry rose; September 25; 2 feet.

POMPONS

Like the singles, the small-flowered doubles are ideal for displays of masses of color, and for other types of landscape work. Averaging somewhat less in height, they combine well in a border with the taller large-flowered doubles; or make excellent low hedges. The colors in this group are especially pleasing when sprays are used to combine with autumn foliage. The Pompons are particularly valuable for Northern gardens because of their ability to withstand considerable frost when in flower.

Early Bronze. Bronze; September 10; 1½ feet.

Early Wonder. Pale pink; September 15; 2 to 2½ feet.

Gleam o' Gold. Glistening yellow; October 5; 2 feet.

Goblin. Bronze; October 18; 2 feet.

Harbor Lights. Luminous creamy white; September 20; 2 feet.

Judith Anderson. Yellow; very free; October 10; 1½ feet.

Mme. Chiang Kai-shek. Bronze; late August; 1½ feet.

Mandalay. Orange-bronze; October 1; 1½ to 2 feet.

Pygmy Gold. Glistening yellow; early August; 1½ to 2 feet.

Rembrandt. Rose-mauve, coppery tints; October 1; 2 feet.

Ruby Pompon. Ruby crimson; October 5; 2½ feet.

Silver Ball. White; October 5; 2 feet.

Silver Tips. Carmine tipped silver; October 10; 2 feet.

CUSHION TYPE

This group gets its name from the dwarf, dense, rounded habit of growth of the plants. This, together with their exceptionally long flowering season, makes them the best of all hardy mums for edging and low masses of color. Also, as a group, they are extremely early flowering, many of them beginning to bloom, under favorable conditions, in July. The individual flowers are not so attractive as those of the later varieties, nor so well suited for use as cut flowers. Despite these shortcomings, they are extremely popular.

Amelia. Light pink, variable; August 15; 1 to 1½ feet.

Apricot Glow. Apricot-bronze; August 15; 1½ feet.

Azaleamum. Similar to Amelia.

Bronze Gold. Gold, bronze tints; September 20; 1½ to 2 feet.

Coral Sea. Salmon, coppery tints; October 1; 1½ feet.

Dean Kay. Better pink than Amelia; August 15; 1½ to 2 feet.

Golden Cushion. Golden yellow; September 1; 1½ feet.

King Cushion. Coppery bronze and dull red; September 20; 1½ to 2 feet.

Lavender Lassie. Cushion Pompon; lavender-pink; September 20; 1½ to 2 feet.

Marjorie Mills. Chestnut crimson; September 25; 1½ feet.

Santa Claus. Hybrid Cushion type; dull red; October 1; 2½ feet.

September Bronze. Cushion Pompon; warm
bronze; September 20; 1½ feet.

September Cloud. Cushion Pompon; white, prim-
rose tinted; September 25; 1½ to 2 feet.

September Gold. Cushion Pompon; brilliant
golden yellow; September 20; 1½ feet.

Summer Sunset. Variable, pink to orange; late
August; 1½ feet.

(Above dates for first-year bloom. Flowering dates
will be earlier in the second year.)

EXHIBITION OR GREENHOUSE TYPE

In this group are included varieties usually
grown under glass, but sufficiently early flowering
and hardy to be managed in the garden under special cultural conditions (see page 98). Unless
such special care can be provided, they should not
be attempted out of doors in Northern gardens. The
varieties suggested below have proven satisfactory
when given the system of culture recommended for
them.

Decorative or Double

Barbara Phillips. Glowing yellow.
Dr. T. N. Leslie. Indian red.
Dr. J. M. Inglis. Amaranth-purple.
Golden Majestic. Golden yellow.
Grace Sturgis. Wine red.
Henry Woolman. Reddish crimson.
Lady Knox. Mauve-pink.

Louise Pockett. White.
Majestic. Amber-bronze.
Marion H. Uffinger. Bronzy crimson.
Thomas W. Pockett. Clear pink.
Vermont. Pink.

Anemone Type

Bob White. White.
Frances Schoen Park. White.
Jeanette. Bronze-buff.
The Titan. Tangerine-bronze.
Tuxedo. Enchantress pink.

Single Type

California Yellow. Bright yellow.
H. Marie Totty. Crimson scarlet.
Improved Grenadier. Red.
Masons Bronze. Burnt orange.
Melba. Bronze red.
Mensa. White.
Sonia. Deep pink.
Stewart Smith. White.

MONTH-BY-MONTH FLOWERING

July. The Cushion varieties Amelia or Azaleamum, light pink; Dean Kay, pink; Golden Cushion, yellow; King Cushion, bronze; Pygmy
Gold, yellow, will flower at this time in their
second year or when well established. Early kinds
should be planted early.

August. To the foregoing add the following kinds which may be expected to flower from mid-August: Apricot Glow, bronze Cushion; Mme. Chiang Kai-shek, bronze Pompon; Milady, orange and yellow; Algonquin, yellow; Seminole, white.

September 1 to 15. All foregoing kinds and Eugene A. Wander, double yellow; Polar Ice, double white; Harbinger, double bronze; Barbara Cumming, double yellow; September Dawn, double mauve-pink; the Pompons Early Bronze and Early Wonder, soft pink.

September 15 to 30. Varieties which flowered in July will now be past their best. Note also that the first hard frost may injure blossoms not yet hardened, particularly white and light pink sorts. Varieties flowering in late September should remain effective into late October.

Double kinds: Avalanche, white; Burma, orange-bronze; King Midas, bronze-yellow; Milky Way, creamy white; Rose Glow, pink; Early Joan Helen, garnet-purple.

Single kinds: Crimson Splendor, red; Hebe, pink; North Star, white; Sappho, yellow; Venus, orchid-pink; Vesta, bronze.

Pompons: September Bronze, bronze; September Cloud, white; September Gold, yellow; Harbor Lights, creamy white.

INDEX

Amateur breeders, 147–48
Anemone chrysanthemums, 50–51
   varieties of, 197
Aphis, 125
Arsenical compounds, 130

Border plantings, 29
Breeders of chrysanthemums, amateur, 147–48
   American, 43–45
Breeding chrysanthemums, 138–65
   hints, 155–57
   mechanics of, 148–50

Cascade chrysanthemums, 51–52
Caterpillars, 126–28
Chrysanthemum arcticum, 53–54
Chrysanthemum breeders, amateur, 147–48
   American, 43–45
Chrysanthemum breeding, 138–65
Chrysanthemum coccineum, 55–56
Chrysanthemum coreanum, 54–55
Chrysanthemum, garden, development of, 36–37
   history of, 34–45
Chrysanthemum, hardy, what is a, 23–25
Chrysanthemum indicum, 35, 57–58
Chrysanthemum, introducing a new, 173–75

Chrysanthemum maximum, 55–56
Chrysanthemum midge, 123–24
Chrysanthemum morifolium, 36, 56
Chrysanthemum, naming a new, 176–83
Chrysanthemum nipponicum, 56–57
Chrysanthemum plantings, 28–31
   for borders
     edgings
     hedges
     masses
     pots
     shrubbery foregrounds
     walls
     window boxes
Chrysanthemum species, 52–58
   arcticum
   coccineum
   coreanum
   indicum
   maximum
   morifolium
   nipponicum
   uliginosum
Chrysanthemum types, 46–52
   Anemone
   Cushion
   Double
   Duplex
   Pompon
   Single

INDEX

Chrysanthemum uliginosum, 57
Chrysanthemum varieties, 58–62
  hardiness of, 60
  recommended, 190–98
  selecting, 58–62
Chrysanthemums, American breeders of, 43–45
Chrysanthemums, Anemone, 50–51
  varieties of, 197
Chrysanthemums, Cascade, 51–52
Chrysanthemums, Cushion, 25–26, 50
  varieties of, 194–96
Chrysanthemums as cut flowers, 86–87
Chrysanthemums, D e c o r a t i v e greenhouse varieties, 197
Chrysanthemums, Double, 192–93
  large, 46–48
Chrysanthemums, Duplex-flowered, 47
  varieties of, 191–92
Chrysanthemums, early-flowering double, 42–43
  origin of, 39–40
Chrysanthemums, Exhibition
  in the garden, 89–92
  in pots, 92–96
  propagation, 97
  varieties, 196–97
Chrysanthemums, garden
  culture of, 63–112
  development of in America, 41–45
  new types of, 38–39
  as pinch hitters, 31–33
  in pots, 111–12
  in South, 88
  in Southwest, 88–89
Chrysanthemums, Hardy, in the garden, 21–33
Chrysanthemums, Korean
  hybrids, 26–27
  origin of, 45
Chrysanthemums, mutations in, 160–61
Chrysanthemums, Pompon, 47–48
  varieties of, 193–94
Chrysanthemums, recommended varieties, 190–98

Chrysanthemums, single-flowered varieties, 190–91
Chrysanthemums, single greenhouse type, varieties of, 197
Chrysanthemums, Spoon, 52
Chrysanthemums, types of, 46–52
  new, 38–39
Chrysanthemums, wintering in greenhouse, 96–97
Cold-frame culture, 109–12
Cultural requirements, 22–23
Culture, 63–112
  cold-frame, 109–12
  condensed rules of, 65–83
  in detail, 68–85
  shade-cloth, 98–108
Cushion chrysanthemums, 50
  type, 25–26
  varieties of, 194–96
Cuttings, propagation by, 133–36
Cutworms, 127–28

Decorative greenhouse chrysanthemums, varieties of, 197
Diseases and insects, 113–32
Dividing, 68–69
Double chrysanthemums, large, 46–48
Drainage, 72
Duplex chrysanthemums, 47
  varieties of, 191–92

Exhibition varieties, 196–97
  Anemone type
  Decorative
  Double
  Single

Feeding, summer, 67, 79–81
Fungicides and insecticides, 128–32

Greenhouse varieties, 197
Greenhouse, wintering not-too-hardy mums in, 96–97
Gypsophila Bristol Fairy, 161–64

Hardiness of chrysanthemum varieties, 60
Hardy chrysanthemums in the garden, 21–33

200

INDEX

Hellebore, 130
History of the garden chrysanthemum, 34–45
Hybridizing chrysanthemums, 150–55
Hybridizing, 142–47
  asters, hardy
  chrysanthemums, hardy
  delphiniums
  dianthus
  hemerocallis
  lupines
  phlox, hardy
  roses
  veronica
  violas

Insecticides and fungicides, 128–32
Insect pests, 116–28
Insects and diseases, 113–32

Korean Hybrid, chrysanthemums, 26–27
  origin of, 45

Leaf drop, 116
Leaf spot, 114–15
Lifting plants over winter, 85–86
Liver of sulphur, 129–30
Location for chrysanthemums, 66, 71–72
Looking ahead, 188

Mass plantings, 28–29
Mendel, Gregor J., 140–41
Midge, chrysanthemum, 123–24
Mildew, 113–14
Month-by-month flowering, list of varieties for, 197–98
Mulching material, 83–84
Mutations, 160–61

Nematodes, 117–23
Nicotine, 128
Non-poison sprays, 131

Paris green, 131
Pedigree chart of double Korean Hybrid chrysanthemums, 184–87

Pedigree chart of single Korean Hybrid chrysanthemums, 183–84
Pinching back, 67, 76–77
Planting, chrysanthemums, 74–75
Plantings, chrysanthemum, 28–31
  for borders
  edgings
  hedges
  masses
  pots
  shrubbery foregrounds
  walls
  window boxes
Pompon chrysanthemums, 47–48
  varieties of, 193–94
Potassium sulphide, 129–30
Propagating exhibition chrysanthemums, 97
Propagation, 133–37
  by cuttings, 133–36
  seed, 136–37
Pruning or pinching, 67, 76–77
Purchasing plants, 69

Records, importance of, 157–59
Red spider, 125–26
Reminiscing, 166–88
Rust, 114

Seed, propagation from, 136–37
Shade-cloth culture, 98–108
Single chrysanthemums, 46
Single-flowered varieties, 190–91
Single greenhouse type, varieties of, 197
Slugs and snails, 127
Smith, Elmer D., 44
Snails and slugs, 127
Soap, 128–29
Soil, 66, 72–74
Soil preparation, 66, 72–74
South and Southwest, chrysanthemums in, 88–89
Spacing of plants, 67, 70
Species of chrysanthemums, 52–58
Spoon chrysanthemums, 52
Spraying, 67–68, 82–83
Sprays, non-poison, 131
Staking, 68, 81–82
Sulphur dust, 131–32

Sulphur, liver of, 129–30
Summer care, 75–79

Tarnished plant bug, 126
Thrips, 125
Time to plant chrysanthemums, 66, 68
Type of plant to plant, 66–67
Types of chrysanthemums, 46–52
  new, 38–39
  two leading, 24–27

Varieties of chrysanthemums, 58–62

Cushion, 194–96
Double-flowered, 192–93
Duplex-flowered, 191–92
Exhibition, 196–97
of greenhouse type, 196–97
list of for month-by-month flowering, 197–98
Pompons, 193–94
recommended, 190–98
single-flowered, 190–92

Watering, 78–79
Whale-oil soap, 129
Winter protection, 83–84